Joseph Remembered

Joseph Remembered

The Father of Jesus

by

Gerald Joseph Kleba

THE SUMMIT PUBLISHING GROUP
IRVING, TEXAS

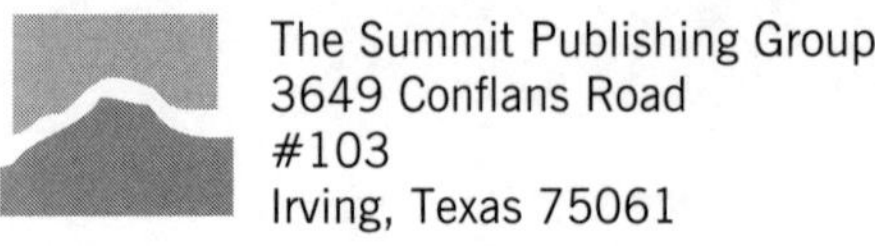

The Summit Publishing Group
3649 Conflans Road
#103
Irving, Texas 75061

Printed in the United States of America

04 03 02 01 00 5 4 3 2 1

Library of Congress Cataloging-in-Publication Data
Kleba, Gerald J.
Joseph remembered : the father of Jesus / by Gerald Joseph Kleba.
p. cm.
Includes bibliographical references.
ISBN 1-56530-307-5 (alk. paper)
1. Joseph, Saint. I. Title.
BS2458 .K58 2000
232.9'32—dc21
00-009817

Cover and Book Design by
D. & F. Scott Publishing, Inc.,
N. Richland Hills, Texas

Dedication

I dedicate this effort to my parents, Phil and Alice Kleba, who loved me into life as the child of their advanced years. Dad was a man of few words who knew that his example spoke volumes. Mom, on the other hand, was quite talkative. She was not shy about telling her children, "You never go wrong when you listen to me."

Secondly, I dedicate this book to Joseph Cardinal Bernardin, the former Archbishop of Chicago. While I met him only once, his life and death have been the best example of lived faith that I have been privileged to witness in this second half of the twentieth century. He referred to himself saying, "I am Joseph, your brother." I am grateful to be related to him.

"Life is a daring adventure or it is nothing."
Helen Keller

Contents

Acknowledgments

I want to thank all of the people who encouraged me and devoted time to this endeavor. Undoubtedly, the person who contributed the most significant amount of time and talent to the project is Helen Smith, a good friend and a wonderful artist who created all of the pictures of Joseph in this book. She created even more than the ones printed here in order to give me a broader selection. Her friend, Jim Trotter, of Color Image, Inc., helped with his computerized artistic talent. His generous and patient assistance was invaluable to me. Among the editors and readers, three stand out for their thoroughness and suggestions. Pam Schaeffer, who suggested that I include more about the daily life of Joseph, Mary, and Jesus. She pointed me to the archeologists who worked on the monumental book published by the National Geographic Society. A huge *thank you* to Bob Sicking, a modern Joseph-like person, and the first editor of this work. As a result of his exhaustive efforts, subsequent editors have had an easier task. I know him well and can certainly attest that in every one of his pursuits, he gives new meaning to the word "thorough." Thirdly, I thank Judy Gruender who continued to make corrections when I thought that all of them had already been made. I thank Tom Taylor for being the on-site computer guru who helped me through many glitches. My sister, Mary Margaret Kleba, and my aunt, Marie Kleba—the wife of Joe, the carpenter—kept encouraging me and were always happy to hear that this work was "still in process." Others who edited the work were S. Ann Fletcher, RC; Julie Harig; S. Jean Meier, CSJ; Patti Barrett; Rosalee Manz; Gil Marsh; Sally Kleba; Barb Hogue; Msgr. Jerome Wilkerson; the late S. Stephanie Vincec, CSJ; Tom Wroblewski; Bert Miller, OFM; John Knoll; and Mark Moloney. Finally, I am grateful for the encouragement of my most consistent supporters in ministry, *The Tuesday Morning Ecumenical Preaching Group*. We have been meeting together to plan our sermons for the last fourteen years. Many of them read this, even when I had feared that they had heard enough of me.

Finally, Bill Scott and Jill Bertolet of the Summit Publishing Group accepted my work and made final corrections and suggestions, bringing it to the excellence of this beautiful publication. To all of them, I express heartfelt appreciation.

Special Recognition

I am deeply grateful to the National Geographic Society for their wonderful book, *Everyday Life in Bible Times*, and especially the section on the flight into Egypt where I heavily depended on that source. I footnoted those ideas and gave proper credit. Without their brilliant explanation of biblical archeology, this work would not be as colorful and alive.

Regarding Art and the Artists

Helen Smith is responsible for most of the artistic representations in this book. The majority of them are original computer art done in cooperation with Jim Trotter of Color Image, Inc. One of them is a photograph of statues that feature Mary as a pregnant woman. This work was done by an unknown artist in the hills of New Zealand. Helen Smith's friend owns the statues and shared this photo with me. A conscious effort was made to have all of the representations of Joseph look different. We hope to encourage the reader to make her/his own imaginary picture of Joseph. Since we have no idea how any of these biblical figures looked, we do not want to impose our view on the reader. Thank you to all of these generous people for sharing in this wonderful labor of love. Each picture is an enhancement to the book.

The cover illustration, *Joseph and Son*, is an oil painting on birch panel by Sister Marie-Celeste, O.C.D., from the Chapel of the Carmel of Reno and is used with permission.

Preface

> "Like Peter (Joseph) we grow into adult maturity by giving up what we have for what we do not yet have on the word of someone who loves us. Like a swinger on some cosmic trapeze, we let go of the bar before the other has quite swung to us and, with our feet firmly planted in mid-air, we trust in the love we have known and wait for the New Life to Come."
>
> *Chaos or Creation*
> Patrick L. Carroll and K. Dyckmen

The cornerstone of my parish, St. Joseph Church in Clayton, Missouri, reads 1900. A devastating fire occurred in 1925, exploding three of the ten stained glass windows that depict the life of Joseph. Although the remaining original windows portrayed Joseph as young and handsome, the later artist insisted on representing Joseph as an old man—bald and gray, with a rustled beard and a furrowed face. Consequently, the replacement Christmas window depicts Joseph at the birth of Jesus looking much older than the original window of Joseph on his death bed. How could this be? What was the intent of the artist?

There are two diametrically opposed notions of Joseph and of manhood in general presented in these windows. I propose that these contrasts are indicators of society's inability to get a clear grasp on what manliness really is. The newer grandfatherly Joseph was chosen in an attempt to display Joseph as a feeble man of weakness and warmth who was putty in God's hand and the recipient of constant angelic inspiration. This Joseph is attractive as a big teddy bear, grandpa person. It is a depiction of Joseph with few redeeming human qualities, the qualities that he taught a compassionate Jesus who would then describe himself as the Son of Man. This was a Joseph who stood at polar opposites with the prevailing notion of a biblical macho man in control and in charge who was free to give his wife a bill of divorce and send her packing. This Joseph, the elder, was an effort to soften the masculine image at a time when men dominated women, who were consequently little more than chattel.

This second artist couldn't imagine a young, strong, handsome Joseph who was also a person of inner strength of character and compassion. He couldn't envision a young man as tender, honest, strong, and fearless; sensitive in relationships without being a wimp. Joseph was the kind of man who knew that compassion is strong and heavy-handed machismo is weak. This perspective totally pulverized the prevailing notion of manhood beyond recognition. I suggest that these contrasts and conflicts fit the current time and the present-day questions about manhood and male role models.

Additionally, I conjecture that this artist feared that a younger, more virile Joseph would never have been able to live a celibate marriage and respect the virginity of Mary, God's chosen woman. Consequently, he painted Joseph as an aged patriarch who was incapable of and/or disinterested in sex. The Bible gives us no clues about Joseph's age except possibly the argument from silence. In the Elizabeth and Zechariah story,

Luke tells us that they are old when she conceived (Luke 1:18). Since the next chapter of Luke's Gospel tells us nothing unusual about the engagement of Mary and Joseph, I surmise that age is not an issue. This being the case, Mary is a young teen and Joseph somewhat older—about twenty.

This book then assumes a vital marriage as a loving relationship that demands sensitivity to a variety of pertinent issues. Not the least among these is the issue of sexual intimacy in their marriage relationship. Allow me to clarify the difference between sexual intimacy and sexual intercourse. Sexual intercourse is physical mating. Sexual intimacy is a sharing of mind, heart, and spirit without physical genital relations. A person who is a healthy celibate, even a virgin, as Mary was, can and should share sexual intimacy in order to be a fully functioning person. There are also parenting matters and openness in the face of self-doubt and failure. Joseph will have to lead his family when times are tough and their child is lost in the temple. He will lose his ability to earn a livelihood in Nazareth during an economic crisis. He will delight in his family when times are wonderful at the birth of Jesus. He will thank God at his death, which presumably occurs before Jesus' public ministry. Joseph is not present at the marriage feast in Cana (John 2:1–11). All of these situations call for emotional stability in joy or sorrow, hugs or tears. Hence, we see a person anchored in a faith that has thrown off fear at traumatic times. Anne Lamott says, "Courage is fear that has said its prayers." Of course, all along Joseph's rocky road of life there is time for prayer and solitude.

Finally, we must confront the notion of Joseph, the father of Jesus. The Gospel writers all refer to Joseph as the father of Jesus. Even though they believed that Jesus was conceived through the power of the Holy Spirit, they referred to Joseph as "father" because they knew the importance of an earthly father. In their culture, men were the pinnacle of God's creation, and the boy Jesus needed a strong, reliable father who offered the security of a good home. For them, the son of Mary was divine and was also fully human.

Some biblical commentators say that Jesus called himself "the Son of Man" to say that he was the fully human one. The baby Jesus, who came to title himself "the fully human one," became such through the fatherhood and nurturing of Joseph. While Joseph was not his biological father, he gave him paternity in every other way. Jesus would teach the disciples to call God *abba*, which means "daddy." He learned the full meaning of that through his wonderful human daddy called Joseph.

I have written this book, *Joseph Remembered,* because the contemporary issue of male consciousness and the men's movement demands this timely biblical approach. Previous books about Joseph have been so spiritual and mystical as to present him as a superman with a direct link to the divine mind. As such, they are out of touch with our shared common humanity. I try to be faithful to the Gospels and make Joseph not Superman, but a super person, who, because of his unwavering faith, walks through a minefield of the sufferings, shocks, and surprises that are our common experience.

Joseph was easily forgotten because the biblical words about him only amount to about two typewritten pages. Since the Gospel writers focused on Jesus and his saving mysteries, they tell us only that Joseph was a just worker, husband, and father. In later history, Joseph was forgotten because his wife, Mary, and his child, Jesus, were so dominant in Christian spirituality. The spotlight that fell on them blinded us to the importance of Joseph in the larger picture. This book is an effort to address this oversight. It jogs the Christian memory. This is not a historical book that chronicles specific events, but rather a story about the human situation of the humble family of Jesus, Mary, and Joseph. While it is not historical, it is based on a true story.

I am grateful to several writers in guiding my search to uncover a more complete picture of Joseph. Several presuppositions have guided me in this endeavor. First, I am convinced that while Jesus was divine, Jesus was also fully human. Joseph, as his father, played an important role in his formative years and upbringing, as does the father of every child. Developmental psychology and family of origin therapy highlight the importance of our generational connections. Joseph left us his legacy in the person of his son. Since we know so much about Jesus, we also know more about Joseph than just the two pages of biblical material.

An old adage says, "The apple doesn't fall very far from the tree." There is also another common saying, "He's a chip off the old block." Jesus is both the apple and the chip, while Joseph is both tree and block. Some backward reasoning and hindsight allow us to understand the role of Joseph. I found Harvard's Robert Cole very helpful in this area. He wrote *The Moral Life of Children,* and tells us about the important role of significant adults in the character development of the young. Many of his subjects attain considerable moral stature despite the fact that they are products of the most abject poverty.

Another lacuna in Joseph's life and the New Testament in general is its lack of descriptive color and physical detail. Certainly, the biblical writers never suspected that people would be reading their works two thousand years later. Presently, we are blessed by all the insights of archeology. We are blessed to know more about the way of life in the ancient world than any other generation. Besides its many articles, the National Geographic Society published a spectacular volume, *Everyday Life in Bible Times*, which proved invaluable.

Joseph is also known through our knowledge of Mary, his wife. What were the tensions and commitments of their married life? What was it like to marry a pregnant teenager? What were the pressures of life on the road to Ain Karim, Bethlehem, and Egypt? What were the reasons behind a celibate marriage? I address all of these and many other important issues. Sally Cunneen has helped me with her book, *In Search of Mary, the Woman and Symbol.* Cunneen might agree that behind every great woman is a great man.

I have enhanced all of these events and issues with my own prayerful reflection on Joseph, my personal patron and hero. In doing this, I have endeavored to put more life and emotion into this great man of mystery. It has been said that humans experience only three things: birth, life, and death. Two of those things we cannot control. The third one, living, is the one we all have in common. Joseph lived an uncommonly whole life. I hope that this presentation of the living Joseph will move him off of the sanctuary pedestals, out of the dim shadows, and onto the center stage of the human drama.

Regarding Jospeh's livelihood, I would like to share with you some of the insightful comments of my editor, Bill Scott.

> The word that is commonly translated in Scripture as "carpenter" actually means something closer to "handyman." Joseph would not have been a carpenter in our understanding, but someone who was experienced in working with tools and had some tools available. We can probably get away with calling him a "craftsman," which still stretches the point a bit. He would not have had a shop where people would come in to buy things, but would have worked on sites when he could for the few wealthy people who could hire craftsmen and would have built things in his home for his neighbors. This work was just a step or two up the socioeconomic scale from day laborers, who actually earned only enough to die, essentially of malnutrition, in five to ten years, but it was not a remunerative way of life. Joseph was one of the poor of the Lord, not just spiritually, but in economic terms as well. We should thus not be surprised that he is no longer on the scene when Jesus starts his ministry. Like most people of his class, he probably just worked himself to death at what we would consider an early age.

Finally, let me acknowledge that those who read this story with a scholar's eye, looking for anachronisms, modern forms of speech, jokes that rely on English, etc., will have no trouble finding them. My purpose was not to describe Joseph's cultural setting with perfect accuracy, but to provide modern readers with an understanding of his character and roles in relation to Jesus and Mary. To do this, I have often felt the need to cast the story in ways that are familiar to our culture, rather than to Joseph's.

Gerald Joseph Kleba
May 1, 2000
Feast of Joseph the Worker

Joseph, the Silent Dreamer

"A blameless life,
St. Joseph,
may we lead,
by your kind patronage
from danger freed."

The Josephites
Baltimore, Maryland

Joseph had dreams
They weren't always clear nor easy
but they were his.
Eventually they changed his mind
And heart.

Not Much is Known of Joseph,
He was Husband, Provider, Father,
Every day
and he had dreams
what more can be said?

S. Madeleva Williams, CSJ

1 Joseph, the Silent Dreamer

Joseph, the boy, was a descendant of the royal family of Kings David and Solomon. He was one of countless many of that lineage over the centuries since David's death. This was a family that had lost its power to the Roman Emperor and the governors whom he appointed to rule Palestine. These descendants of monarchs and world leaders were not even figureheads. The great dynasty was barely a memory. However, they also still symbolized hope. Among the faithful Jews, there was the promise that some day the Messiah would come. He would be of the royal family of David.

There must have been only a spark of hope for a boy named Joseph, born to parents of so little fame that their names are forgotten even to legend. Joseph was such an unheralded lad that he would be counted among the *anawim*, the Poor People of the Lord. These people had little status, popularity, prestige, education, property, or importance. These people were truly humble.

The words *humble* and *human* come from the same Latin root word, *humus*, which means "ground." Truly humble people are humans who are well grounded and people of the earth. They are "down to earth folks" or folks with their "feet on the ground." These people are

not self-exalted. They are lowly and humbly aware of their broken humanity and their need for God. They recognize their limitations. They don't know it all or have it all together. Since they are people who can laugh at themselves, they might say, "I have it all together, but I forgot where I put it." They know and understand reality and understand suffering as well as any people on earth. They know that they are only passing through this world. They are frail and fleeting. While rocks and rivers have millions of birthdays, humans only have a few and then bid the world farewell. Throughout the Bible, God shows a preference for insignificant people, a commitment to raise up the lowly and humble the haughty. This was the experience of Israel and of Joseph, the silent. He was a humble human who was truly one of the Poor People of the Lord.

When Joseph was a boy, his father told him the great stories about God and the enslaved Hebrew children. He told him about Moses and the Pharaoh and about Joshua and the tumbling walls of Jericho. He told him about David, the shepherd-king, and his son, Solomon, with the understanding heart. He told him about the fidelity of Ruth and the love of Miriam for her baby brother, Moses.

No matter how many of those great old stories he heard, one was his all-time favorite. It was the story of Joseph, his ancestor, being sold into slavery. His jealous brothers could not stand the special treatment that he received from their father. Presenting Joseph with an expensive coat was the last straw. However, in his imprisonment, Joseph turned this nightmare into a dreamy situation that got him out of prison and allowed him to be the one who controlled the food in Egypt and saved his family from famine. Joseph heard all of the stories, including some of the tales of sin and chicanery that were also a part of his family. Alas, no one comes from a perfect family.

Many of these revered ancestors led lives marred by infidelity and selfishness. There were David and Bathsheba. There were Solomon and his harem. There was the stealing of Esau's birthright by Jacob. Joseph's dad told him about God's ways for people who were always acting too big, too important, too stubborn, and too proud.

One story that Joseph relished and remembered was the story of the great flood and how Noah, the mythic hero, saved the human race and the animals by building an enormous ark. After hearing that story at bedtime more than any of the others, Joseph decided that he, too, wanted to be a craftsman and help people by building and repairing things they need. He learned some other virtues at story time, as well. He wanted to be a quiet and attentive person so that he could even be awake to his dreams like Joseph of old, who forgave his traitorous brothers and repaid them by saving his family from famine in Egypt. He wanted to be fair and honest rather than a liar and thief. He wanted to be a faithful husband to one wife rather than a philanderer and a playboy. Joseph's father often told him that life always presents a person with two questions, "Where are you going?" and "Who will go with you?"

Joseph's family was not wealthy. His mother always told him, "Be grateful for what you have." She taught him to count. At the same time, she taught him to count his blessings. As he learned to count up to ten, each number had to be accompanied by a blessing. One, Grandma. Two, Eyes. Three, Ears. Four, Hair. Five, Fingers. Six, Sunshine. Seven, Nose. Eight, Mommy. Nine, Daddy. Ten, Toes. As he counted higher, he learned to add a blessing for each successive number. His mom would say, "Joseph, God is so good that you will run out of numbers before you will run out of blessings."

She would also say, "Remember this Joseph! Wealth consists not in having many possessions, but in having few wants." Since Joseph had very few toys and a simple home, he knew that he would have to count the gifts of nature as his most valued possessions. Those things that nobody could own were the things that he prized the most. He could lie on the grass for hours and imagine fantastic scenes in the designs of the clouds drifting across the blue skies. He could study a day lily close up and marvel at its delicacy and its toughness as it was buffeted by the breeze, even though he was fully aware that it would be dead tomorrow. He knew the cooling refreshment of raindrops on his tongue. But most of all, Joseph could treasure a tree. Trees gave shade. Trees gave fruit. Trees gave songs in the gentle breezes. Trees gave wood for fires and for carpentry. Trees gave homes to the birds and the squirrels and even to people. Joseph loved to look at streams and brooks, rocks and rivers, clouds and drizzle, flowers and finches. Most of all, Joseph loved to look at trees. As a boy he would run across the meadow to sit under his favorite tree. He felt empowered by its unyielding strength.

Joseph liked to watch his father work with wood. It was his calling in life to develop the same skills as a craftsman. For more generations than even the oldest patriarch could remember, the men of Joseph's family had been village handymen and craftsmen. Since trees were scarce in their homeland, each one was prized. The wood that was used to fashion furniture, fixtures, cutting boards, and tool handles was selected for durability and treated with tenderness. Like a jeweler cutting fine diamonds, Joseph's father wasted little.

Often when Joseph was watching his father at work with the chisel, plane, or saw, he would ask questions such as, "What kind of wood is this? Where did it come from? Why do you use it to make a hoe handle? Who made the tools? How do you know how much to charge for a chair?" Sometimes his dad thought he was raising Joseph the "curious" craftsman.

At other times, Joseph would talk of his dreams. He cherished Joseph, the Dreamer, as his hero. He was proud to be named after a person who was clever in dream interpretation. He admired Joseph's prison release and befriending by the Pharaoh for his understanding of dreams. As a boy, Joseph tried always to remember his dreams. He was very happy when his father would lay down his tools and listen to his dream stories. Sometimes they were scary, and sometimes they were strange. Always his father listened and, now and then, offered an explanation. Sometimes the best thing was to offer a secure hug when the dream was particularly bizarre. He never could have dreamed how his dreams would change his whole life.

God the creator of all things, you have imposed on all men and women the obligation of work. May the example and prayer of blessed Joseph help us to accomplish the tasks you have commanded us to perform so that we may attain the reward you have promised through our Lord Jesus Christ, your Son, who lives and rules with you in the unity of the Holy Spirit, one God forever and ever.

Joseph the Workman, Pray for Us.
Maryknoll Sisters
Maryknoll, New York

Perhaps the Mark of Greatness is not the accomplishing of Great Moments, Great Monuments, Great Works;

Perhaps the Mark of Greatness is Facing Life as it comes, being content with the daily, what we call ordinary;

Joseph was that kind of a person, a man, a Saint.

S. Madeleva Williams, CSJ

2 Joseph, the Craftsman

> He came to his hometown and began to teach the people in their synagogue, so that they were astounded and said, "Where did this man get this wisdom and these deeds of power? Is not this the carpenter's son? Is not his mother called Mary?" (Matt. 13:54)

From childhood on, Joseph knew what he would be when he grew up. He didn't have the kind of choices that later generations have—of becoming an archeologist or a botanist or a cartographer, much less a zoologist. He didn't have the choice of going from A to Z in a college catalogue. His father's father was a craftsman in the tiny village of Nazareth, and his dad had followed that same path. So this father's son would be a craftsman also. The choice was pretty much made at birth, because that is what family and tradition dictated in those days long ago. Opportunities for a person to strike out on a new path were rare.

Joseph's father had told him when he was very small that the smartest person is the one who enjoys his work. When Joseph was in his teens, his father made this notion abundantly clear. He said, "Know

how to find one laugh for yourself every day, for one laugh is better than a jug of wine! Hear a joke every day and laugh, or make up one of your own if you can. Just find something going on that seems funny, and then laugh and say to yourself, Joseph, start whistling a tune, and keep laughing, and tell yourself you're still alive, and you'll be alive tomorrow. Beyond tomorrow no one knows." (Coles, 104–105)

Joseph felt blessed to grow up in a family where his thoughtful father was like an artisan. Every tool in his father's hand was as special to him as a paint brush in the hand of Michelangelo or a plane in the hand of Nicholas Stradivarius. Craftsmen at that time did not make the ordinary, crude, or simple items that any peasant fancied he could make. Rather, they crafted such things as the yokes that were custom fit for the oxen and the plows that would open the furrows for planting in the arid, slow-yielding terrain of Palestine. Oxen were fitted for yokes in a way that respected the unique contours of their shoulders so as to guard against abrasions and chaffing. The process was trying and required patience and endless fittings. An animal that was injured by a poor fit could require rest and recuperation right in the middle of the plowing or harvesting. In contrast, a well-designed yoke rode easily and even a huge burden was considerably lightened.

The building of plows also required a sophistication and mathematical accuracy that was beyond the abilities of the peasant class. This was the setting in which Joseph grew up. He had been such an adept student of the craft that he devised some modern improvements, which he molded into the plow with his loving, capable hands. Had he lived closer to the Mediterranean Sea or the Sea of Galilee, he might have stretched himself so far as to become a master boat builder. Others who were similarly talented found boat building a lucrative livelihood, but it was not to be for Joseph. (Brown 539–40)

Joseph's skill in his craft was matched by his kindly disposition and personal integrity. He was a tall, strong man whose muscles rippled with even the slightest motion. He carried himself in a proud, confident fashion that was the obvious bearing of old nobility. His uprightness also applied to his character, which could be both stubborn and soft. Joseph learned from his father the art of people skills and the meaning of honesty and integrity. He believed in paying a fair price for the lumber he bought and in asking a reasonable price for the plows and yokes that he produced. Joseph was a man of straightforward simplicity who respected others and was aware that special situations called for special consideration. Each person had a unique story, was a unique person and, thus, deserved unique treatment. It was no surprise when the Nazareth natives nicknamed him "Joseph the Just."

Joseph said his way of doing business demanded four considerations. First, pay help fairly. Secondly, treat customers with integrity. Third, contribute to the betterment of the community, and lastly, make a profit. "If I make a profit without doing the other things, I don't deserve my nickname," Joseph contended.

There is a story told in the Talmud. A man arrives in a town, looking for someone who can solve a problem. He asks the people whether a rabbi lives there. On

receiving a negative reply, he asks: "Is there a carpenter among you, the son of a carpenter, who can offer a solution?" (Levy, 338). This seems to indicate that the craftsman in a hamlet like Nazareth was the best qualified person for questions concerning the *halakhah*—the Jewish law. As such, Joseph was a paradigm of thoughtfulness and virtue. He was the village craftsman and holy man.

When Diogenes was carrying a light everywhere he went, people asked him what he was looking for. He replied, "I am looking for an honest man." He would have stopped his search when his gaze fell on the face of Joseph the Just.

Joseph, the Husband of Mary

St. Joseph, you found God
in simple things—
a dream or two, a carpenter's trade,
a woman you loved,
an unborn Child, a growing Boy.
Open our hearts' eyes and ears
to the God in our daily lives
and open our hearts' hands
to bring God's loving touch
to a world of persons in need.
Sister Mary Ann Hilgeman, CSJ

3

Joseph, the Husband of Mary

The marriage of Mary and Joseph was undoubtedly arranged by their parents. Joachim and Ann are the names traditionally given to Mary's parents. Because they were very holy people who had gone to the great effort of raising their daughter as a prayerful person, they were looking for a husband who would treat her with honor and respect. Joseph, the craftsman and widower (see appendix), was a prime candidate in their parental matchmaking. He was a man of proven integrity, respected for his craft, and even more renowned for his character. Joseph may have been a head taller than any of the men in the village, but most of the people there looked up to him for more than physical reasons. Secretly, Mary's friends talked and giggled about her great good fortune. Joseph was handsome and seemed to maintain a youthfulness that belied his true age. Aside from some smile lines, he was the picture of trim energetic youthfulness. Surpassing all else was a radiance that signaled unmistakable holiness. Mary was the envy of all her girl friends who hoped that they would fare as well. More than anyone ever knew, this was a match made in heaven.

When Joachim and Ann arranged the engagement, Mary was delighted and eager. She knew Joseph would love her and needed her as the mother of his children. They were James, Joses, Judas, Simon, and their two sisters. (Mark 6:3). The sad, early death of Joseph's first wife had been noted and mourned by all in the tiny village. Mary was the right woman with the ideals and energy to tackle the awesome challenge that this marriage would present. The marriage date was fast approaching. There really was no marriage ceremony. The day would come when Joseph would arrive at Ann and Joachim's house and bring the donkey that he agreed to give them in exchange for a daughter. He would get the blessing of her father and lead her to his home as his wife. Then the party would begin. This simple transition would be celebrated with a lavish party for everyone in Nazareth. Mary had already spent considerable time getting to know and care for Joseph's eager brood. Happily, Mary was succeeding in ways that far surpassed the hopes of any young woman who would try to replace a dear mother who died too young. Then an abrupt intrusion rocked this comfortable, placid scene.

"In the sixth month the angel Gabriel was sent by God to a town in Galilee called Nazareth, to a virgin engaged to a man whose name was Joseph, of the house of David. The virgin's name was Mary. And he came to her and said, 'Greetings, favored one! The Lord is with you.' But she was much perplexed by his words and pondered what sort of greeting this might be. The angel said to her, 'Do not be afraid, Mary, for you have found favor with God. And now, you will conceive in your womb and bear a son, and you will name him

Jesus. He will be great, and will be called the Son of the Most High, and the Lord God will give to him the throne of his ancestor David. He will reign over the house of Jacob forever, and of his kingdom there will be no end.' Mary said to the angel, 'How can this be, since I am a virgin?' The angel said to her, 'The Holy Spirit will come upon you, and the power of the Most High will overshadow you; therefore the child to be born will be holy; he will be called Son of God. And now, your relative Elizabeth, in her old age, has also conceived a son; and this is the sixth month for her who was said to be barren. For nothing will be impossible with God.' Then Mary said, 'Here am I, the servant of the Lord; let it be with me according to your word.' Then the angel departed from her." (Luke 1:26–39).

If the angel Gabriel thought Mary was frightened when he began his presentation, he should have stayed around long enough to see her cold sweat after his disappearance. She was stunned, dazed, and drained of energy as she slouched back in her chair and wondered what this encounter was all about. One might describe her pale and puny demeanor as "limp as a dish rag," but that would really be giving her credit for some semblance of control and composure. As she tried to reconstruct the apparition and remember every phrase and gesture, her head was spinning out of control. She was saddened to think that she did not remember it all and also disappointed when she thought of all the good questions that she failed to ask. Yes, she had asked the biological question: How was this to be? She secretly hoped that Joseph's fatherhood would be the answer to that question. But now that the mental whirlwind had subsided a bit, she was disappointed that she had failed to ask some other important questions. Was Gabriel planning to make a similar appearance to her parents and to Joseph and even to the local rabbi, chief priest, and town gossip? She would certainly feel relieved if she knew that was in the master plan. It was maddening for her to think of all the best questions when it was too late to ask any of them. The right answers would surely leave her much less vulnerable and afraid. She knew that she really couldn't assume anything. On one hand, she could kick herself for her thoughtlessness, but then she was so stunned and the incident was so brief. On the other hand, she was proud of her simple acquiescence. She knew that this had been a deeply spiritual encounter and that she had been correct in saying, "Let it be done as you have said." As startling as it was, the situation was most certainly a meeting with the Holy One if it wasn't a dream. While there were unanswered questions in this faith walk, Mary was confident that she was indeed on a providential path. She also felt proud to be counted as worthy and highly favored. When God had previously chosen people, like the prophets of old, they all had their excuses. Mary just said "yes."

Now there was the question about the right way to approach her parents. They had always said that she could feel free to talk with them about whatever was on her mind. As reassuring as that was, Mary was indeed reluctant to talk with her parents about the angelic message. She was confounded by every aspect of its profound implications. As a virgin, she was embarrassed to talk about pregnancy at all. Cautiously and with a red face, she began to tell her parents. Soon it seemed her red face was contagious and Ann and Joachim began to blush also.

They were astounded to hear of this incident. What was the meaning of all this? Should they proceed with the marriage? Ann burst into tears and hugged Mary. Joachim sat and stared. While on one hand her angelic encounter was mind numbing, on the other hand, there was a certain family calmness. Mary had always been a girl graced with radiant joy and loving openness. There was always a wonderful aura of unfeigned kindness on her face, and she was the picture of peace. While parents would never expect divine intervention in their child's life, Joachim and Ann might have been the exception. Mary was always a special girl of inner peace and refreshing innocence. Lastly, there was a sense of pride and relief in hearing Mary divulge the final response in her dialogue with the angel. "Let it be with me according to your word." She manifested faith and openness that surpassed the wildest imaginings of even her parents. *Exceptional* was really the only adequate word to describe this teenager. Even at the tender age of five, she had loved to talk to the rabbi and made her charming presence felt. She cherished her private time to listen to God. Simply stated, Mary liked to pray. She was also eager to meet new people, even if one happened to be the angel Gabriel. However, one especially puzzling question that Mary asked drew a blank from both of her parents. "What did it mean when the angel told me that the Holy Spirit would come upon me? Who is the Holy Spirit anyway," she asked with wide-eyed innocence?

Neither Ann nor Joachim was in any hurry to answer, because neither of them had ever heard the term before. Finally, Joachim admitted his ignorance. "All I can think is that the Spirit of the All Holy hovered over the water at the time of creation. I just don't know, but I do believe that you had some type of holy experience, and anything that is holy has some connection to the Lord. But I don't know, because all of us Jews are proud to be monotheists." Then he opened up the issue and asked, "Ann, have you ever heard anything about the Holy Spirit?"

Mary's mother simply shook her head in stupefied silence. After all, women were not expected to have answers to theological questions. Other husbands would never have asked a woman's opinion. Holy Spirit was a non-word to her also. In an effort to be more participatory, Ann changed the subject to an upbeat notion that she could relate to more easily. "It certainly is good news to hear that Elizabeth and Zechariah are finally going to have a baby. I bet that they are the happiest people in town, and I am sure that all of the towns folk are delighted along with them." Now there was a simple and joyful comment that broke the tension and brought a momentary smile of relief to everyone's face.

Joachim and Ann joined her in planning the best way to approach Joseph with the earth-shaking news. It occurred to them that the village busybodies might count the days until their daughter's first child was born. Ann concluded that some small-minded people always need to talk about other people. Mary and Joachim practiced role playing to give young Mary a bit more poise and confidence in the daunting task that lay before her. How would she share this with Joseph?

On the very next day, a lazy afternoon, Joseph came to visit at Joachim's house. It was a hot summer day, the children were all playing, and Joseph decided to quit working early. No breeze was stirring and neither were any of the town's people. Joseph was free to visit Mary at her house since he was widowed and well-respected. Not all of the details of pre-wedding etiquette applied in their case. On the preceding night, Mary had lain awake praying and rehearsing her story. She decided that this was the time to pop the news and tell Joseph the details of her angelic visit.

She refilled Joseph's goblet with some water from the big pottery jar standing in the shade of the north side of Joachim's house. She put the jar back on the rough-hewn table and came to sit by Joseph on the uneven stones of the porch wall. She cleared her throat and began.

"Joseph," she began in a high-pitched, nervous voice. "I have something to tell you that is going to be hard for you to understand. I know that, because this is hard for me to understand. I'm still in a daze, and the incident that I'm going to describe happened to me."

Mary paused, and Joseph moved closer to her on the wall, took her hand, and interrupted. "Whatever it is that you have to tell me is all right. I'm sure that I will understand," he said confidently.

"Now just promise that you'll listen and not lose your temper, and be patient until I'm finished, because this is hard," Mary pleaded.

"Why, when have I ever lost my temper with you?" Joseph countered somewhat indignantly. "Now I'm really curious. What is it that you have to say that is so hard and has you so upset and worried," Joseph queried?

Mary composed herself and began the story. "Joseph, you know that I try to pray each day. Well two days ago I was praying. I was right over there in the corner of the room. I was kneeling back, sitting on my feet with my hands on my lap and my eyes closed. I was over in that corner of the room where the lamb's wool rug covers the earthen floor. I was thinking about the Creator's goodness and remembering the first verse of the psalm that reads: 'Happy are those whose way is blameless, who walk in the law of the Lord.' It was a time of peaceful bliss when I felt a surge of energy flowing through my body, and I was excited about being alive. In fact, I don't know if I have ever felt more alive. Then without any kind of warning and with my eyes still tightly shut, I saw this vision of an angel, beautiful and in flowing purple, dangling in mid-air before me like an orchid hanging from a graceful green stem. Before I could even embrace the unexpected beauty that appeared out of nowhere, I heard a voice speaking to me. I didn't know if I should open my eyes and if I did whether that would spoil the moment. The voice knew my name and said, 'Hail Mary.' Now I was shocked and quivering, and I could feel the blissful energy leaking out of me like water from a cracked vase. I had goose bumps and I was perspiring all at once. It seemed like my mind was full of sparks or lightning, and my heart was in my throat.

Even as she retold the story, her voice was beginning to get soft and her mouth dry as felt. Joseph tried to reassure her and urged her to continue. "Mary, this is exciting. Please go on with your story."

"Well, Joseph, listen closely. This is where it gets very hard to tell and to believe. First, the angel told me to calm down and fear not. Well, that was easier said than done, because I was shaking and anxious and verging on tears. Then, the angel told me that I was a grace-filled person who had been especially chosen by God for an important task. I know that others called by God said, 'No, not me, I'm not worthy, I'm inadequate.' But I never said those things. Then, get this Joseph, and please don't faint: He said that I was to bear a son and name him Jesus. Gabriel, that's how the angel introduced himself, said that this baby would be the Son of the Most High. Now I knew why he told me not to be afraid. I was so sacred that I shook and my teeth chattered. I can't tell you how startling this was after the shock of the beautiful vision. So I asked how this was to happen since we were not yet married. The angel said that the Holy Spirit would come upon me and that all things were possible with God. What do you suppose that 'Holy Spirit' title is referring to, Joseph?"

Joseph just sat there and looked at Mary with stunned skepticism. He couldn't even respond, but beads of perspiration were now forming on his reddened brow. He was sweating more profusely than when he was working with his tools.

Mary continued. "Joseph, I hope that you are still with me. I told you that this would be hard to say and hard to hear. You just have to believe that it was a shock to me and wasn't music to my ears. For a while, the angel who said his name was Gabriel just stared at me like he was waiting for me to come back with an answer of some kind or another. I thought about asking another question, this time about the Holy Spirit, but then I thought that I'm young and a girl at that, so I probably don't know everything that I should know about God. But then later on, I asked my parents, and they didn't know about the Holy Spirit either. My father knew about the spirit being over the water in the creation story in Genesis, but that didn't seem to connect with my situation. Then as a kind of afterthought, this Gabriel person said that my cousin Elizabeth was going to have a baby, and that as old as she is, anything is still possible for the Almighty. Well I guess that's good news, because everyone wants to have heirs. I just wonder how she's going to make it at her age and if Zechariah is able to help her very much."

After a long pause, Joseph gathered enough strength to respond. "Is that the end of the episode? Did the angel just disappear after that," he asked?

"No, the angel just kept floating there, and even when I opened my eyes, he was still there right in the living room inside the door there. Slowly, a response formed on my lips, and I said: 'Here I am, take me for God's work.' Come inside and I'll show you the exact place and then you'll know as much about this as I do." With that, she pulled Joseph to his feet and ushered him into the house—to the corner by the front window and the hearth.

They stood in the very spot where the apparition occurred, and Mary finished her account. "There was just one more thing. Since the angel kept hovering there and I felt so shaky and foolish, I finally asked if there was anything else. Gabriel said that he was waiting for my reply. All I could say was, 'Let it be as you have said.' I barely had the words out of my mouth and the angel disappeared as quickly as he had entered the scene. Here's where I stayed, shaking, drenched in sweat, tears on my cheeks, and feeling the weight of a mountain on each shoulder. I couldn't even move from the spot until my mother returned from the well. Then she saw me looking so bleached and stricken that she imagined that I was sick. But strange to say, once I settled down I felt joy, maybe even excitement, with the beauty of the setting and the compliments of the angel. Joseph, now you've heard the whole story. What do you think?"

As Mary concluded her mysterious presentation, she watched the life drain from Joseph's face. He became ashen and quizzical. The veins began to protrude from his forehead, and the artery pumping up his neck throbbed almost to the breaking point. He was so taken aback by the story and its consequences that he was frozen in his place and at a loss for words. His original enthusiasm for the angel had waned, and he was in his own state of shock over Mary's evaluation of the situation. If he heard right, he knew that she was expecting a baby through such incredible circumstances that the story challenged the entire belief system of this faithful man. Mary felt a great sadness sweep over her and felt cold rejection after she shared her story. Over the past two days she was once again openly energized with great joy and unaffected innocence. But now Joseph was shut down with strained disbelief. She was so transparent in her goodness and candor that Joseph was caught totally off guard. He had only come for a

cup of water and to share a friendly chat while he wiped off the beads of perspiration. He thought that he would cool off, but instead he had been struck by this bolt out of the blue. He could do nothing but excuse himself and stagger away like a drunkard. He turned away shaken and sullen with his eyes sunken into their sockets. He had no response but to leave the half-empty cup, because he was too upset to even stomach water. Streams of sweat were rolling down his face and back while he shivered with a cold chill on this steamy afternoon. He could hardly believe his ears. Mary was going to have a baby. His ears burned, his head throbbed, and there was an ache in the pit of his stomach.

Before he returned to his own home, Joseph arranged with relatives to keep his children for the night. They saw his bewilderment and asked him if there was anything wrong. He grunted something indiscernible and kept walking. Joseph would have to think and pray and agonize over a situation he never thought he would have to face. Mary stood in the shadows of Joachim's doorway with streams of tears rolling down her cheeks and her face so pained she thought it might crack. Is this what "let it be done to me" meant, she agonized? Would it be a lasting separation?

Joseph was righteous, a strict observer of the Mosaic Law. He could have nothing to do with this questionable situation. Since they had not yet come to live together, his first thought was to call off his marriage to Mary. He could divorce her quietly, but the children would certainly balk and ask a hundred questions. He paced, he turned, he sat, he got up again and then threw himself across his bed in exhaustion and drenched the mat with his salty tears. Another horrible question arose that he dare not allow to surface. It was too scary. If Mary were accused of adultery, would she be stoned? He pressed his eyes tightly closed, trying to make the image disappear into the darkness, but the weighty question persisted. At first his sleep was fitful, but then he fell into a sleep as deep as a coma. Only death itself would have been calmer. The angel appeared to him in a dream and said. "Joseph, son of David, do not be afraid to take Mary as your wife, for the child conceived in her is from the Holy Spirit. She will bear a son, and you are to name him Jesus, for he will save his people from their sins." (Matt. 1:20–21). He awoke from his sleep drenched in perspiration once more, but now he was relieved, alive and excited. In fact in those few hours the agony was ended, and he, too, knew an inner calm and peace.

As Joseph pondered this new twist on a shattering situation, he received an answer to his query. In fact, the Holy Spirit gave him a profound insight. In the Roman world where male domination was so pervasive, and in Roman colonies where soldiers casually raped women, God was bringing this child, His Son, into the world without the standard male cooperation and intervention. The ordinary and assumed masculine power and control fell aside in the face of this divine plan. God would intervene and totally undermine patriarchal prominence and prestige. Joseph breathed deeply and humbly assented with a wordless silent nod. He exhaled. As soon as the first hint of light broke the sky, he was back at Mary's door, wearing a warm and knowing smile. Her story, which had initially taken him to the depths of despair, now bolstered him to blissful heights.

In her sleeplessness, Mary had spent the night telling her parents and reliving the angelic event. The shock of Joseph's quiet departure left her flustered and disheartened. It totally deflated her and brought the entire relationship into question. But at the first light of dawn, they heard the steps on the flag stone path. They knew that it was Joseph and cautiously welcomed him to the family meeting. Try as they might, it was difficult to pretend that nothing had happened yesterday. Joseph apologized for his hasty departure the previous evening. His lips quivered uncontrollably as he fought back tears and begged the pardon of everyone. He even admitted that maybe he was resentful and jealous of Mary's holiness and special call. He began talking with a glint in his moist shiny eyes. "My angel came to me in a dream last night. He was nameless, but let's call him Gabriel." Joseph smiled. Mary and Joseph looked into each other's eyes and laughed. "My situation was simpler than yours, but it still left me scratching my head. I had already heard your story, so the angel and the baby were easier to accept." They giggled freely, like mischievous youngsters.

Joseph told Mary of his dream and his continuing desire to marry her. He was relieved and was more thrilled than ever to have her as the mother of his family. "I love you more than you will ever know," he whispered into her ear softly but proudly. "Do you still love me after I walked out in a huff?" They looked into each others eyes and smiled and gave each other a gentle hug. Since Mary and Joseph had both come to this mysterious awareness of God's plan through the mission of an angel, neither one of them could do anything but praise God and move forward with their marriage plans. Somehow, God would see to the details of this mysterious web. Their job was to be open and joyful in the present moment and the future promise.

Wedding Feast

On the day of their marriage, none in Nazareth would have suspected the strain and misery that they had suffered just a few days earlier. The person Joseph ushered from Joachim's house was the most beautiful bride anyone in town had ever seen. Mary was a remarkable creature with the darkest eyes, thick brown hair like her father's, and a Mediterranean complexion. She wore a fine blue dress with a tucked bodice shaped by the smallest suggestion of a bosom. And Joseph escorted her proudly, followed by a string of children. As the town feast began, Joseph was his most ebullient self. He talked incessantly and laughed with such vigor that all the people around him wore constant smiles on their faces. It was a celebration the villagers would not soon forget.

Joseph knew that taking Mary into his home meant more than just a geographical change of location. In the Jewish mind, it meant consummating their marriage. But he was hesitant about that aspect, because he knew that there was something especially pristine and wonderful about this woman who seemed almost angelic herself. As good as she was, humble Joseph saw himself as an undeserving partner and even a mismatch to Mary, God's chosen one. On their first night, he was frightened and could not bring himself to having sexual relations with Mary. Instead, Joseph spent the night in prayerful pondering. He knew that God

only intervened in a person's life for one of two reasons. Either a person may be facing such an awesome mission in life that God had to make his presence felt, as was the case with Abraham or Moses at the burning bush. Otherwise, God talked to a person who was so bad that he needed a jolt to save him from falling into the clutches of the evil one. In all honesty, Joseph didn't see himself or Mary in that second category, but he questioned whether he was being called to a vocation as high as the patriarchs. He asked himself what might be the purpose or the price demanded by this call. God was certainly recognizing Mary and secondarily calling him to participate in this holy parenting. When he considered it in the most simple and straightforward fashion, he thought: God has chosen Mary and placed her on a pedestal. Somehow Joseph was to stand beside her.In this marriage, Joseph would be God's best man.

As he prayed, it became clearer to him. If God had impregnated Mary with his powerful Spirit, Joseph must respect this holy tabernacle and treat it as untouchable and as unapproachable as the Burning Bush on Sinai and the Holy of Holies in the Jerusalem Temple. He must never consummate this marriage and presume to lay claim to Mary, because she had already been claimed by God's Holy Spirit. So Joseph had taken Mary home on that marriage night, but not in the way that most Nazarenes imagined. Joseph was a God-fearing man and aware of his own nothingness in comparison with the greatness of God. Joseph was thrilled with his new wife, a mother for his children, and content with his own call to second-fiddle servanthood.

On the following morning, Joseph shared this revelation with Mary. She listened with rapt attention and accepted it with blushing innocence. They would have more time to consider it in all of its ramifications. They suspected that it would take a lifetime. Right now, however, Mary had other concerns. She wanted to go and visit her cousin, Elizabeth. Joseph would be a single parent again. The angel had mentioned that Elizabeth was expecting a child in her old age and was now in her sixth month. Surely, this was a sign that could confirm their own situation.

Joseph had never anticipated these travel plans, but he knew that he could not stand in her way. He knew that given his familial responsibilities, it was impossible for him to accompany her. The home of Elizabeth was in Ain Karim, ninety miles to the south of Nazareth. Joseph was deeply concerned for Mary, a teenager, traveling from one hamlet to another with not much of consequence in between. While Joseph could not accompany her, he could not deter her. He helped her plan and pack and tried to radiate confidence and put aside all of his worries. Joseph had a deep trust in the Lord God and a deep trust in life. Certainly, if God were to give them this beautiful opportunity for service, then God would take care. If the angel had not wanted Mary to take such a risk, then Gabriel should have cut the announcement short and skipped the information about Elizabeth's pregnancy. If Mary had not known, she would have stayed at home and started to make baby clothes. But since she knew, there was no question but that she would go and fuss over her elderly kinswoman, whom she would only now meet for the first time.

Joseph refused to be sullen or selfish. He helped Mary find some traveling companions so they could head south together. There was more security in numbers. He knew that the roads would be hot and dusty, and some of the plank bridges would be rickety. Packs of wild dogs were known to roam the area on occasion. He knew that there could be sickness along the way. Joseph envisioned the trek and knew that a person could live with a compound fracture—but a ruptured appendix? Joseph didn't even bother to finish the thought. He knew that she could die from fatigue, hunger, and exposure. He would rather have amnesia than think of brigands and gangs. All of that was a harsh possibility, bitter medicine to swallow, but it was reality. He had already lost one dear wife, so he was no stranger to death.

Mary had her walking staff and her loaded pack. Joseph fought back the tears. They finished their prayer together and gave each other one more warm, lingering embrace. While Joseph was still kissing her forehead, Mary turned quickly and set off to join the party of eight strangers on the rugged road. Ever since the call of Abraham, all of God's people had to leave their creature comforts and face risks. Reluctantly, Joseph returned to his home, worked on a wheel, and dreamed daily dreams of cuddling a new baby. At least it was a beautiful day, and Joseph was cheered by the large white clouds that moved briskly under the clear blue sky.

The first one hundred days of their marriage were spent at a distance, but always united in spirit. Finally,

Mary returned home safely, and Joseph exhaled. With the dust of the wilderness still on her clothes, Mary began to blurt out all of the details of the trip. She was brimming with news of their new cousin, John, even as her own pregnancy was beginning to show. She had all the news to share about her long unseen cousin, Elizabeth. The biggest news revolved around Elizabeth's wonderful greeting when she opened the door to Mary, who was exhausted from the trek. When Elizabeth heard Mary's greeting, the child leaped in her womb. And Elizabeth was filled with the Holy Spirit and exclaimed with a loud cry, "Blessed are you among women, and blessed is the fruit of your womb. And why has this happened to me, that the mother of my Lord comes to me? For as soon as I heard the sound of your greeting, the child in my womb leaped for joy. And blessed is she who believed that there would be a fulfillment of what was spoken to her by the Lord." (Luke 1:1–45).

Joseph listened to Mary as she told this beautiful story, and then both of them beamed with the joy that they found in each other's eyes. There was also great curiosity about the new baby whose promised arrival was surrounded by mystery. The news was that John's birth had been normal and ordinary and with the help of a mid-wife proceeded quite smoothly for a woman of her age giving birth to her first child. Its angelic announcement had caused a doubting Zechariah a prolonged silence, but Mary was happy to announce, "You should have seen the neighbors when he began to talk after he wrote the words, 'His name is John.'"

What would be significant about their child who was announced by the Angel Gabriel and conceived by

the power of the Holy Spirit? Would there be fireworks or an eclipse surrounding his birth? Would he glow in the dark? The questions were unanswerable. This time of separation had been a time of endless questions and wondering. The answers would only come in the daily living and the years ahead.

Apparitions and dreams had preceded their marriage. Awake or asleep, questions haunted Joseph. What is the meaning of this dream? Is God intensely interested in a simple craftsman and his wife? Does the All Powerful God depend on the lowly and powerless? What is God's plan anyway? These were just a few of the questions that had floated through Joseph's mind during those busy days and lonely long nights without Mary. They surfaced amidst his constant concern about Mary's health and safety. The questions allowed no answers, only speculation. Joseph knew that being a widower was rough, and marriage to Mary wasn't going to be easy either. He also knew from the scriptures that many of God's chosen wished at times that they had been overlooked.

When Joseph allowed himself to overwork, he became even more confused and impatient. That was a sure sign that he needed to relax, go for a walk, or visit a friend. At other times, he found a quiet place in the shade, sat down, calmed himself, and listened to the birds sing. In the stillness, he could hear the voice of love with each breath. Joseph had heard a rabbi once say "An undisciplined mind goes wild while a disciplined mind finds peace." He was blanketed with a warm inner peace and a confidence that God's mysterious plan did actually involve him and his young wife, Mary. Ah! Sweet serenity! It was out of that realization that he would be able to approach Mary on her return from Elizabeth's house with a new idea.

When all the news had been shared, Joseph broached the new idea he had conceived during Mary's absence. He suggested, "I've been thinking that we should try to refrain from sexual relations throughout the duration of our marriage. I already have children and know that experience. I think that God has a unique first claim on your body as the expectant mother of Jesus. I think you are marked as a chosen temple of holiness. I could never feel worthy as a sexual partner." Mary was aglow with relief and excitement. She fell into his arms in an enormous bear hug. This was the very same inspiration that she had received as she walked those long miles on the dusty and dangerous road. They agreed that it would be difficult because their love was unrelenting, but they would do it one day and one night at a time. Her body would always be the special sanctuary of the Holy Spirit.

This commitment would call for the greatest human determination and the total guidance of God's grace. When Mary questioned Elizabeth's pregnancy, the angel Gabriel said, "All things are possible with God." Mary and Joseph would be assured of God's providence in their lives also. First and foremost, it would have to be a life of prayer. They would have to go to the synagogue regularly and celebrate the holy days and festivals at home. They would have to invite God into all the places in their work and their public and private lives. They would have to join hands for ten minutes of shared prayer every night and recommit themselves to their marriage and their celibacy on a regular basis.

This would be their best time to share the thoughts, feelings, joys and troubles of their day. They would have to become one in every way but the carnal way. Finally, both Mary and Joseph would have to have some solitary quiet time to listen to the Lord.

They would have to be alive and responsive to the needs of their children and others in the community. In that way, neither would fall into the trap of living life as if it were a pity party, moaning, "Oh poor little me. Think of everything that I give up. I wonder if anyone else endures this kind of pain and disappointment, suffering and sacrifice?" They would have to find time for feasts and celebrations. The lives, birthdays, and achievements of Joseph's children would have to be marked appropriately. Each holy day would have to be prepared well and shared with family and friends.

Finally, the life that Mary and Joseph were called to lead was one of great tenderness and intimate caring. It had to be a life of physical closeness and great concern about the feelings of each other. If there were any displays of temper between Mary and Joseph, they were reserved for arguments between themselves and almost never revealed to outsiders. They must be reconciled before bedtime. Before embarking on this extraordinary way of life, Joseph talked to the wisest rabbi in all of Galilee, who told him the value of hugging. "Hugging is healthy. It cures depression, reduces stress, induces sleep. It's invigorating. It's rejuvenating. It has no unpleasant side effects. Hugging is a miracle food. It is organic, naturally sweet, and one hundred percent wholesome." Joseph wrote this saying on his tool box:

"Life requires four hugs a day if you want to be healthy and seven hugs if you want to grow."

Chaste living required particular compassion in the midst of sickness and suffering. Each had to be able to see the other as beautiful and worthy of the utmost respect as a child of God. They would have to be particularly sensitive when the other person was the most vulnerable, needy, and forlorn. At those times, they would have to be cognizant of the saying, "Beauty is in the eye of the beholder." Otherwise, they would not be able to look at the other at all. The love between them had to be so total that there wasn't any room for lust.

Reflection

Joseph is the patron of working parents, adoptive parents, foster parents, and stepparents. Do you know any parents who ought to get a big hug and a "thank you" today in honor of Joseph?

Prayer

Loving God, You have put your faithful servant, Joseph, in charge of your household. You put your Son, Jesus, in the care of Joseph. Put us also in Joseph's care. Let him watch over the whole church. May he remind us to share what we have with the poor. We ask this through Christ our Lord. Amen.

Song for Father
Omar McRoberts

Long ago, a father or fathers
would take sons into
dark trackless woods and ruff
them up a bit, teach them laws of
Society and Universe, teach them
Mysteries of Manhood. I
remember no such night journey, yet I
know that over
years I
have undergone silent, powerful
initiation with you, Father.
For in your example, I
have found seed of mysteries.

You have shown
Paradoxes of Right Action and
Selfless Giving. You have given gentle
Wisdom and Peace of mind.
And you have shown hidden art of
Introspection:
only art which can
save world from Itself.

Father, you offered truths to me in a
night journey of years and I
emerge from darkness with thirst for
Mysteries
more awesome consuming than even Manhood.
Father, you have shown sacred art, and I
thank you.
Father, you have put seed of Thirst in me—-
and for this, Father,
I love you. (McRoberts, 251–252).

4 Joseph, the Forgotten Father of Jesus

The Birth of Jesus

Joseph and Mary were almost accustomed to dreams and angelic appearances when another shocking intrusion jolted their life. This came in the form of a Roman decree. Mary was resting from her long and taxing trip to visit Elizabeth. It was the eighth month of her pregnancy, and she was already beginning to prepare a place for the new baby to sleep. The news raced through Nazareth like a spark through stubble: Caesar had ordered a census, and everyone was to go to his ancestral hometown and register. How could this be? It couldn't be scheduled at a worse time. But those were Caesar's wishes, and there was nothing that anyone could do about it. Caesar's wishes were law, and his subjects had to obey.

And so, instead of resting her weary body and her aching feet, Mary needed to pack for another grueling trip. Joseph would have to work nights to get the straw mattress stitched tightly for the new arrival. Fortunately, the older children were helpful and even excited about the prospect of a new baby brother. Since they were old enough and relished the chance to stay home

alone, Mary and Joseph had no qualms about leaving them. They were "alone" with extended family all around. Many hands made the work easier even though the days were few and pressure packed. Joseph advised his eldest son, James, to keep an eye on both the household and the business. He should be especially attentive to his younger siblings during their brief absence. There was a completed oxen yoke that had to be delivered to a local farmer as soon as possible. The farmer would bring the oxen for a final fitting.

The seventy-five-mile trek from Nazareth to Bethlehem was less lonely and dangerous than Mary's venture to visit Elizabeth and Zechariah. Neither the road nor the destination were as solitary at the census time. There were other people from David's line making the same journey. Still, there were dangers from sickness and starvation, brigands and bandits. There were deserts and ridges and miles of desolate land. There was the crippling coldness of camping under the stars and starless nights that were darker than a thousand midnights. Sometimes there was a shortage of water. A parched mouth and chapped lips were an agony. They were confident they would survive; in fact they would thrive, because they were eagerly awaiting their new arrival. It was a time to wonder and not to worry. They continually prayed the psalm that read: "Protect me O God, for in you I take refuge." It was a time for prayer so deep that Joseph almost fell into a walking trance. Mary's donkey ride was miserable but tolerable. For the poor, especially mothers, pain is a given in life, and complaining merely wastes energy. It never changes anything.

Joseph's prayer nurtured his faith and gave him the confidence and hope to keep on trudging with Mary at his side and God's angels above. The wind, grit, and dust in this arid land belied its title as "the land of milk and honey." In fact, the degree of filth was sometimes as high as the degree of temperature on the sun-baked desert at high noon. Finally, they stumbled like zombies into Bethlehem to find themselves homeless. The hometown of King David rolled out no red carpet for a craftsman whose wife was pregnant. The cost for a room at the Bethlehem Inn was inflated by the crowds, and all the rooms were filled. Bethlehem was small and unaccustomed to large crowds. Mary's labor pains were beginning. Her contractions were becoming more regular.

Fortunately, the kindly innkeeper told them about a cave on the outskirts of Bethlehem that was often used as a stable by the local shepherds. In their desperation, the forlorn place seemed almost comfortable. They settled there for the night. The frenzy of the moment was complicated by the darkness and the embarrassment of their situation. Joseph was anguished over the fact that he could offer his new bride so little comfort and security. In fact, they had enjoyed very few days together since they were first married. Life was out of control, the way it frequently is for people who say yes to God's way. Besides that, they were hungry, but all the stores charged outrageous prices for the meager food that was available. They would have to make do.

But the hunger was forgotten when it happened: Mary's water broke and the baby was coming quickly. At least this had not happened on the road in the middle of nowhere. They might have been nobodies, but at least they

were somewhere. There had shelter of sorts. There were sticks and a fire pit. There was a stone manger with hay. There was a stream and a bucket. And they were two of the most in love people under God's heaven. Hastily, Joseph built a fire while Mary endured the pain and fear that has always been a part of childbirth. She was drenched in the perspiration of labor and shivering in the chill of the night. Only one side of her was warm—the side closer to the fire.

Mary's belly throbbed as she pushed and grunted and perspired. Then Joseph caught the baby as he slithered out of the birth canal. And then they were three. A baby! A boy! A son! A hope! A star!

The baby yelped his first cry and split the silence. The pain was forgotten. It was not Joseph's first experience at being a dad, but it was his first experience at being a midwife. In just two weeks, Mary would mark her fourteenth birthday. Mary and Joseph looked at each other and the baby as Joseph laid him on her breast. There were lumps in their throats and tears streaming down their faces. Their hearts pounded with inexplicable joy. Was the light and warmth in this dank, dark place from the stars or from their starry eyes? Joseph took the baby and bathed him, rubbed him with oil and salt to harden his muscles, and then wrapped him in swaddling clothes. Joseph laid him on Mary again, and the flicker of the fire caught the tears of joy in their eyes and on their beaming faces. Later, Jesus was taken by Joseph from his mother in a formal ceremony of fatherhood. Taking the child on his knee, he proudly affirmed the boy's birthright in the family of King David. For a moment, the stable became a castle fit for a boy king.

Something tremendous had happened that was beyond the ordinary birth—if indeed there is such a thing as that. However, the demands of living in such a rudimentary and comfortless place denied them the time to reflect on the moment. Warmth and a modicum of comfort for Mary and Jesus were the immediate concerns. Joseph gave Mary a little kiss on the cheek and then turned his attention to heating some water. The blessing of the cave was not merely the shelter it provided, but more especially the shepherds who came home that night to find the family of intruders. All that Mary and Joseph lacked, the shepherds were eager to provide. While their appearance was dark and rough as the wilderness from which they had emerged, their demeanor was one of tender caring.

That day for the shepherds had been long and blessedly boring. No wild animals had confronted or molested their flock. Aside from a burning wind out of the south that had left their faces raw, it had been uneventful. And just as they were about to put the herd to bed and head for the protection of the high-walled canyon with its cave, the black sky lit up with an apricot glow. The sheep began to panic with wide-mouthed fright and throaty, choked bleating. A voice as resonant as the herald in the king's court bellowed: "Do not be afraid." It echoed down the canyon.

The more the angel announced it, the more afraid the quaking, cowering shepherds became. They studied the fright in each others eyes and knew that they would feel better facing a young lion. The voice continued: "See, I am bringing you good news of great joy for all the people." The modulation and richness of the voice was hypnotically soothing. “To you is born this day in the city of David a Savior, who is the Messiah, the Lord. This will be a sign for you: You will find a child wrapped in bands of cloth and lying in a manger."

Then as if perched in the sky on airy, invisible risers, angel choirs appeared without warning. They hovered against a stage curtain of columned clouds colored like the Northern Lights. A silent swish, like the updraft of a hundred ascending eagles, was followed by a deafening stillness. Poised in the night sky, still as hummingbirds in formation, their flowing garments were as colorful as the rainbow. They were human in shape but devoid of real form. They were colorful transparencies. Their number must have been fifty, and their sound filled the valley with a melody hitherto unheard on planet earth. With a sweeping motion from the angelic conductor, they sang praising God:

> "Glory to God in the highest heaven
> And on earth peace among those whom he favors!"

When the angels had left them and gone back to their heavenly abode, the shepherds said to one another, “Let us go now to Bethlehem and see this thing that has taken place, which the Lord has made known to us." So they went with haste and found Mary and Joseph and the child lying in the manger. When they saw this, they made known what had been told them about this child; and all who heard it were amazed at what the shepherds told them. (Luke 2:8–18).

They were good shepherds who lived for their sheep and were ready to lay down their lives for them. They were shepherds who knew how to care for helpless lambs—newborn, breathing wool balls—when their mothers had been killed or injured by critters. They were also good at caring for helpless people such as refugees with a baby. At first the young couple was scared by the rustle of brush and the poor bleat of a goat in the north wind. But when they watched the flock following their shepherds into the cave, they were comfortable and relieved of the scariness of the lonely unknown. Some of the braver sheep went further back, exploring the darker, lower recesses of the cave. The smaller lambs stayed with their mothers or close to the shepherds, because they knew that they would be safe and warm there. Mary and Joseph welcomed the intrusion and proudly showed their sleeping newborn to the visitors, who marveled and sang soft lullabies or entertained with baby talk goo-goo words. The welcome visitors seemed to also bring some of the angelic light and warmth with them. Joseph had been concerned that Mary might catch a cold, but now there was a warmth that seemed to go beyond the heat of the fire and the flock. It was the warmth of friendship.

The shepherds told Mary and Joseph about the amazing light and the musical announcement they had witnessed concerning this birth as they were moseying to the sheep gate. Then Mary settled down from her excitement and fell asleep on the pallet the shepherds provided for her. Joseph was holding Jesus and glowing with a pride that could not have been matched if the new baby boy had been his own. As they all became more comfortable together, Joseph told his mysterious story. There were reflections and shadows from the flickering fire lighting his face as he spoke about the angelic messages that had interrupted both of their personal lives. There was a common angelic

connection that brought a comfortable joy to these newfound friends as they all struggled with the novelty and the ordinariness of this birth.

While the cave was not as comfortable as the Bethlehem Inn, there was a sort of coziness about it. People at the inn were making a vacation of their trip and having noisy parties. Joseph and Mary were simple people with a newborn who needed a less raucous setting. Some of the party people might have viewed new parents with a baby as wet blankets on their festivities. The situation with the weary shepherds was more serene. Among the shepherds in the cave, they were *family*. The prices in Bethlehem were exorbitant, so this perspective made a virtue of necessity.

Mary slept on as Joseph breathed easily and found comfort enough to cuddle their child. He was a miracle—living, kicking, and crying. The soft illumination of a ripe Judaean moon danced on the humble surroundings as Joseph bowed down in awe at life's primal miracle. Jesus' white swaddling blanket shone in the light, but he didn't glow in the dark. In his tight wrap, Jesus was very cozy and comfortable. Mary's nap was all too brief, because soon he was crying to be fed and changed.

After a fitful night of napping and nursing, Mary was wide awake at the crack of dawn. She was dirty and disheveled from the trip and the labor, but she was radiant with joy and excitement over her new bundle of life. Joseph was sound asleep on the hard, cold ground, and the fire was a mere single, smoking ember. Mary pulled her blankets tightly around her and slowly got to her feet. She woke up Joseph to rekindle the fire. Usually it was the woman's job to tend the fire, but Joseph was not bound by most of those traditions and was eager to help as needed. Both of them knew that nursing a crying infant was a more urgent task—and one that the baby demanded on his schedule, not theirs.

The shepherds were up washing their faces and getting some breakfast. They invited the new family to share their humble porridge of wheat groats with some cucumbers. It was an extremely ordinary breakfast for people whose lives the previous night had been so extraordinarily divine. In the spirit of family, they all sat around a common bowl and dipped in with their right hands.

As Mary and Joseph observed these unremarkable surroundings in the light of day, the lead shepherd took center stage and began to lay out a plan of action for the day. "Today is the day to take care of the census. We shepherds decided that we would be able to help you with that task." He pointed to a boyish looking fellow and continued. "Micah will go with Joseph into Bethlehem and try to pull some strings. He has a wealthy uncle and his father-in-law is the rabbi. They can take Joseph to the census officials and avoid standing in line with the crowd.

"Now, as for you young lady, new mother," he smiled and bowed deeply with a gesture of respect to Mary, "this is our plan for the home front. Solomon, the wizened veteran, will shepherd his flock close to the mouth of the cave right here where we are sitting. Whenever he circles his flock, he will stop by to look in on Mary and the baby to see if everything is all right. He also has a sheep dog. If there is a problem, Ole Shep will go off for help from some of the other shepherds in the

area. That will allow Solomon some time to give a helping hand and Mary to have some rest. That dog of his is so fast and fearless you almost have to pity the wolves if any should attack. Sadly, the grass is a bit thin and matted in this area because of the regular traffic, but the sheep won't starve in one day. The needs of the new mother and baby boy are much more pressing." He paused for a moment to recollect the plans and reached down for another slice of cucumber.

"If everything goes well today, all of the important things should be accomplished. Then tomorrow when the census work is completed and Mary has gotten a chance to catch her breath, we will move the young family to my house in town. That way they will be safe and secure, and we can celebrate with them until after Circumcision Day. After that, we can make further plans depending on how well Mary and the new baby are doing." The head shepherd seemed quite content with the thoroughness of his agenda for the next week, and he sat down again to finish his breakfast.

As the shepherd spoke, Joseph's mind wondered about the events of the recent past. He thought, even though there was the assurance of the angelic promise, thank God the baby is a boy. How much better than a girl, who would leave home and is therefore a "false treasure!" But at least even girls were not disposed of, as often happened in Egypt or Rome. He knew well why Jewish men began their morning prayers by thanking God that they were not born a woman.

For a week the family celebrated as the honored guests in the shepherd's home. On the eighth day, the village *mohel*, a specialist, circumcised the child. In becoming a Jew, the boy received a name, usually his grandfather's. (Nat. Geo. Soc., 304). However, this case was different. The name had been designated by the angel, Gabriel. (Luke 2:21). Joseph would have the honor of naming this special child Jesus.

The Visit of the Magi

Joseph and Mary had hardly recounted their blessings of cave, shepherds, security, home and family when camels carrying impressive and statuesque wise men lumbered into town. They arrived from far-off Persia. They were so flamboyant in their gold, purple, and crimson as to be a regal sight. They glided in on the swaying camels with a hushed silence that made them appear to be a mirage of mystery men. Camels were an uncommon sight grazing Bethlehem's sheep and goat pastures. Even more extraordinary were the colorful and majestic visitors who wore funny looking pointed hats and from whom luxurious gold and purple fabric flowed opulently. Servants and livery men hovered around them like the angels had over the shepards. The rhythmic swagger of the camels seemed to be a fitting accompaniment to the regal elegance of their riders. There were some circumstances surrounding the birth of Jesus that were difficult for Joseph to comprehend. The magi ranked almost as high as the angelic visitors.

They inquired about the presence of a new baby at the house where a huge quasar had positioned itself. Joseph rushed out to see the commotion. The visitors introduced themselves and then proceeded to explain, "We are stargazers." One simply stated, "We search the vastness of the heavens looking for portents for our

people. When we spotted this new star that was so lustrous and diamond-like, we knew that it had wondrous significance." What sounded earthshaking to Joseph was matter-of-fact to the visitor.

"We are Persians, Magi who have come from a long distance east of the Tigris, where snow-tipped mountains gleam against the sky. We worship the one true god as taught by the prophet Zarathrustra."

Joseph had never heard of that prophet, but the visitors' presence was impressive. Joseph listened carefully, not knowing what to think. Bewildered as he was, he did know one thing for certain. Hebrews generally damned the art of astrology and put it on the plane of idolatry. But these men were such gentlemen and had come such a long way to see his son that he felt drawn toward the prevailing virtue of hospitality. The Hebrew children had once been strangers in a strange land and had longed for refuge.

Melchior, Baltassar, and Caspar had been studying the sky one night as was their custom. This night there was a new constellation and a star bright beyond the brightest of the stars. It beckoned to them and called them like the sweet singing of an ancient siren. They had no more choice about this trip than the Nile had about flowing northward. It was nearly a compulsion. It was time to follow the star that was so bright and dominating that it might be announcing the arrival of a king—the King of the Jews.

The congratulations and protocol that usually surrounded worldly wealth seemed to be unnecessary for these three. They were humble, thoughtful, and congenial amidst their opulence. All the while deeply dependent on their entourage of servants. The gifts that they brought were surely impressive, indeed nothing short of dazzling. The contrast between life in a stable and gifts fit for a king left Joseph and Mary pleasantly baffled. First, they presented a fine wooden chest brimming over with gold of every description from coins to nuggets to exceptional jewelry, including an exquisite filigree broach. Joseph had never seen so many gold chains, medallions, and bracelets in his entire life. He could not imagine that all the shops in Jerusalem had a collection as large as the display presented to him. The temptation was to abandon his work. Joseph the artisan saw the polished wooden jewelry box as one of the brightest gems among the treasures presented. It was certainly a king's ransom. The frankincense seemed to be as spicy and aromatic as any he had ever inhaled in the confines of the temple. Those privileged to offer temple worship to the all high God longed for such a rich fragrance. It was an aromatic delight after living in a sheep pen birthing area.

Finally, the myrrh seemed to be such an odd and unseemly gift. The embalming spice was so out of place for the birth of a tiny infant. It certainly had a fatalism about it that no new parent wished to consider. But there they were, such fine unexpected gifts from such impressive visitors that no questions were asked. A gift is a gift, but these were treasures from foreigners. Maybe the deeper meaning was unclear, but the meaning of a gift is universal.The entourage of visitors and their gifts represented an interior bowing of the heart before Davidic royalty.

Mary, Joseph, and all of Bethlehem were called to festivity and celebration by the surprise visit of the foreigners. For their part, the Magi had been equally shocked by the ignorance and apparent disinterest of Herod and his Jerusalem court. Melchior told the entire story at a village festival welcoming the foreigners. Hospitality was *the virtue* for any true follower of Abraham. So often, Yahweh's people had to depend on others for food and safety on a pilgrimage. Through these ordeals, they learned that God comes disguised as a stranger so one must always be hospitable. The town festival was quite lavish. Even the mayor and rabbi gave the visitors a formal and lavish welcome. But anything the Bethlehemites did paled in comparison to the treasures the Magi had lavished on the newborn King of the Jews.

Melchior thanked those who assembled and assured them that the biggest gift he received there was the opportunity to meet and greet Jesus, Mary, and Joseph. Then he told about how they had lost track of the star near Jerusalem and stopped to inquire about the birthplace of this great one. They strode up to Herod's Palace and were greeted with respect and deference. The decorum of the court attendants was very refined and well rehearsed. They knew that their robes and their camels were great curiosities. However, once they presented their question about the newborn King of the Jews, they could feel the tension, coldness, and suspicion mount. Herod barked questions to his courtiers and magicians about this newborn and met a wall of blank stares in return. Then he sent a message to the temple demanding the immediate consultation of the high priest and his entourage.

In the next hour, the high priest and his scribes appeared before Herod, but in the meantime Herod disappeared from the audience chamber. From the moment when the question had been asked regarding the King of the Jews, a look of shock and hatred masked Herod's face like a doughy crust. Angered and infuriated, he rose from his high-backed leather chair and paced back and forth, staring at the floor. He paused as he considered the hokey story of a star. He raised up his wine glass and gulped it. He slammed it back on the marble table with such force that he broke the spindly stem and the crystal glass splintered on the floor, spilling the last swallow. This only precipitated more anger, and his bulbous nose flared with a road map of tiny veins. Then he disappeared out the door to the balcony, calling his general to fall in step with him.

"We just sat there stunned and abandoned as this scene unfolded," said Caspar. "Clearly, Herod was not as enthusiastic about that new star and its meaning as we were. Finally, the Jewish high priest arrived from the temple. There were a half-dozen priests and scribes tagging along with him. They were ushered in quietly and a page went out to the courtyard to call Herod and his general. Herod climbed the five steps to his throne as the high priest and his entourage stood at attention at the foot of the platform. In a gruff and raspy voice, he barked at us. He ordered us to recount once more the appearance of the star. When we had finished retelling our story, he turned to the Jewish leader and bellowed, 'Well, what do you make of that new star, esteemed high priest?' His voice dripped with sarcasm.

"The Jewish leaders had a quiet, intense huddle and after a few minutes the high priest cleared his throat and spoke up. 'According to our reading of the holy texts, the Messiah should be born in Bethlehem of the family of King David. This is the exact quote as it is written by the prophet:

> And you, Bethlehem, in the land of Judah, Are by no means least among the rulers of Judah; For from you shall come a ruler Who is to shepherd my people Israel.' [Matt. 2:6]

"'That is all that we know, but this much does seem very clear: Bethlehem is the city where a ruler is to arise. But there really is one more thing that I must point out,' the high priest said. 'My faith compels me to be this honest even at the risk of embarrassing these wealthy travelers. Our faith warns us about false gods and teaches us that astrology verges on idolatry. Hence, I strongly doubt that anything in God's plan is going to be revealed to pagan stargazers and magicians. That is the most absurd and preposterous thing that I could ever imagine. Consequently, I would take all of these imaginings with a grain of salt. I think that our esteemed visitors might just be moon struck from looking at the sky too long.' He smiled and rolled his eyes to indicate a judgment of lunacy on the visitors, even as he glanced over to Herod to avoid eye contact with the guests. 'In my humble opinion, it would be best for these Magi to turn around and go home.' With that, he folded his arms smugly and stepped back from the royal platform looking like a chief justice handing down a decision."

Everybody at the town festival laughed at the self-deprecating comments that Caspar shared so candidly. When the keys to the city had been presented and the treasures of the Magi put on display at the town square, many folks shared in the festivities of eating and drinking until the wee hours of the morning. Hardly anyone could recall a more elaborate affair or a better spirit of hospitality and community pride. Bethlehem had not hosted such important personages in centuries. Several of the synagogue leaders were shaken by the idolatry comment and chose to withdraw from the celebration quietly. Everyone else wanted to get a chance to give the Wise Men a traditional greeting. It was an unusual cross-cultural celebration—unseen in such a small, backward village.

The children were intrigued by the awesome size of the Magi's camels; however, the adults maintained some distance because of their horrible smell. Of course, the children all begged to take a camel ride, and the livery men were given strict orders to oblige any youngster who prevailed upon them. They were intrigued by the way that the camels got down on their spindly knees and allowed the passengers to walk right into the saddle. The camel's strength, stature, spitting and stench became legendary to people who had never imagined such a strange animal existed.

The joy of the celebration and the reverent attention that the Magi paid to Joseph's family was a highlight of the brief visit that ended too soon. In a private conversation with Joseph, Baltassar mentioned an aspect of the encounter with Herod that they never shared at the public celebration. He noted that Herod had a parting comment just before they left Jerusalem. Herod asked them the exact time that the star had appeared and then he told them, "Go and search diligently for the child; and when you have found him, bring me word so that I may also go and pay him homage." (Matt. 2:8).

Baltassar continued: "I never mentioned this on the night of the big party, because I thought that there might be some Herodian spies there. However, I was curious about the fact that Herod was so interested in personally looking for this child. I didn't know if he was up to any good, but I just found it interesting that he was so intense, infuriated, and curious. Then last night I had a dream that we should go home by a different route and not return to Herod or tell him anything. Maybe that sounds odd, but that's what happened. What do you think of that, Joseph?"

As a smile warmed his face, Joseph replied, "Baltassar, I must tell you that I am a strong believer in dreams. If that's what you heard, then I say obey and don't question it. You don't have enough time now to hear all of my dream stories, but I'll tell you this much: I've had several important dreams that have all proven to be true. So don't doubt your dream for a second. Another thing that makes this dream authentic is the fact that the Herod you saw fretting and fuming is a tyrant and a bully of the first order. Believe me, he is curious and he is cunning. He responded to your questions because he was disturbed at the news you brought about the birth of a child who might be important, indeed, one who might be competition. Since he was intrigued by your news, he listened to you. That news and the fact that you are rich got his attention. Otherwise, he is such a ruthless cutthroat that he might have been content just to kill you, steal your treasures, and enslave your servants and stable boys. You are searchers and seekers led by a star. He is a total materialist who carries the trappings of the Jewish faith but is not really Jewish and is led solely by passion and power. For him to kill a person, even a family member, is about as inconsequential as crushing a cockroach. While many people value happiness, Herod is happy with hostility. One image captures him perfectly. He is religious on the surface and would never kill a pig or eat pork. But he has killed several of his own sons who were handsome and charismatic and hence possible competition for the throne. He also killed his wife. Some people have said that they would rather be Herod's pig than Herod's son. In view of that, I would encourage you to go east by traveling west if you must, but listen to the dream. Stay away from Herod and don't go back to Jerusalem."

The Flight into Egypt

For a few days, this sleepy hollow had become the town that never sleeps, but with the departure of the Magi, Bethlehem took a nap. However, the frenzy would not soon be forgotten. There was still a bit of hubbub when folks gathered at the well and recalled their visitors' lavish outfits, or when their children boasted about petting the camels. Some argued about who had the longest camel ride. Mary and Joseph knew that it was time to pack up their baby and their treasures and head back to home and family. The census trip had been greatly extended, but the hospitality of the shepherds and the wealthy visitors had been an unanticipated pleasure. The excitement of this month had been so special as to almost make them forget Nazareth. But there was also a family that they dearly missed and which was always on their mind. They merely had to trust that they were safe since all communication was impossible. Mary and Joseph mused quietly that tomorrow would be departure day, and the shepherds had done much to help them prepare for the return trip.

On the night before their departure for Nazareth, Joseph had another dream. It reminded him that his earlier dream had been preceded by Mary's angelic visitor. His dream was readily believable, because it mirrored the astrologer's dream. The voice said, "Get up, take the child and his mother, and flee to Egypt, and remain there until I tell you, for Herod is about to search for the child and destroy him." (Matt. 2:13).

Joseph remembered how he had described Herod to the Magi and sat bolt upright in bed. He was breathing heavily, and his heart was racing as he recalled Herod the Horrible. Mary was awakened by his groan and the rustle of his sleeping mat. She asked him if he was having a nightmare. He explained his dream and then debated the urgency and immediacy implied by the words, "Get up, take the child and his mother, and flee to Egypt, and remain there until I tell you, for Herod is about to search for the child and destroy him." After a few minutes of shaking the cobwebs out of his groggy head and then reviewing the dream with Mary, he decided that the middle of the night was the right time to depart.

They roused their host family and began to do their last minute preparations. One minute they were treated like royalty, and now they were leaving in the dead of night like hunted outlaws on the run. They arose and dressed to the light of a half moon and a feeble wick in a pottery lamp. Joseph was happy to buy a pack animal from his hosts with some of the gold coins. He also was able to buy a few wine and water skins that would be a necessity in the arid lands that awaited them. Mary was wrapping Jesus for the next leg of the journey that was to go in the opposite direction than they had intended hours earlier when they had shared a good-night kiss. Joseph was strapping their possessions on the donkey, while Mary was wrapping Jesus in swaddling clothes to protect him from the night chill. They had a tearful farewell with the shepherds, whose hospitality had been their best birthday present. Jesus was four weeks old and was beginning to smile.

As Joseph did the packing, he recalled the stories of his childhood. A thousand years earlier, Joseph had been sold into Egypt by his jealous brothers. Eventually he would save those very brothers from the seven years of worldwide famine. Now, this Joseph was on his way to Egypt too. He silently questioned the scary situation and, at the same time, wondered if it was a journey into exile all over again. It was an odd situation for him and Mary, but they had come too far not to believe in voices and dreams. Joseph helped Mary onto the donkey and hoisted Jesus into her lap. They were humble people on a simple animal making another unplanned journey in the wrong direction. Joseph hoped he was right with God.

Their late-night beginning was bleak and treacherous, but by early morning they had reached the campsite of a caravan on its way to Egypt. They fell in with the group and were relieved with the newfound hospitality and company. Danger and adventure promote bonding. This trip was luxurious in comparison to the

Jerusalem journey when Mary had been pregnant and funds were skimpy. Now they had a pack animal and a healthy mother nursing a happy baby. And thanks to the Magi, they had money in their knapsack and treasure strapped to their donkey and wrapped in dirty laundry to keep it hidden. Joseph carried the bulk of the gold in a purse strapped around his waist. The God who draws straight with crooked lines was taking them on another circle tour. All they could say in unison was, "Let it be done." Mary had used the line originally, and now it was becoming their life mantra.

The trade routes between Bethleham and Egypt were busy and better services were available to those who had money. When they arrived in Egypt, they were happy to find a small Jewish community that had returned to that fertile strip of land seven hundred years after Moses had led the Hebrew children to the promised land. They welcomed the small new family and offered hospitality to Mary and Joseph that matched the kindness of the Bethlehem shepherds. Since they had the money from the valuable gifts, they were able to live like tourists. Many of the women of the village were eager to take care of Jesus while the curious couple visited several exotic sites.

Egypt was full of excitement for Mary and Joseph. They got in touch with their roots, beginning with Joseph's sale into slavery. The Egypt that Mary and Joseph encountered was much like the Egypt of their ancestors. It was a strip of green real estate, the "gift of the river" lining the Nile, for some six hundred miles. The river drew scarcely a drop of rain from the bright skies; in Egypt no tributary brought it waters. The burning sun and thirsty sands drank its moisture. Yet here in this valley, people had settled thousands of years earlier when grasslands withered on the plateaus and game became scarce. The Nile's surging summer floods enriched Egypt's soil with layer upon layer of alluvium from the heartland of Africa. Now Joseph could stand with one foot on the fruitful black soil laid down by the river and the other on the lifeless sand of the desert. Proud Egyptians called their home the "black land" and themselves "the people." Sea and desert walled off their land from potential enemies. (Nat. Geo. Soc., 107).

As they toured, they heard proud Egyptians explain the big picture. As Stone Age farming villages grew into cities, then provinces, separate kingdoms of Upper and Lower Egypt gradually emerged. About three thousand years earlier, the kingdoms combined into a single nation under an all-powerful god-king.

If the Nile River were not enough of a prize, they also visited the pyramids, which their ancestors built without straw but with large doses of their own tears and blood. Beginning with the early dynasties, great pyramids rose—wonders of the world in any age, symbols of the yearning for immortality and of the power, skill, and organization of the Egyptian state under its kings. (Nat. Geo. Soc., 108).

If Egyptian scribes recorded the Hebrews' escape on papyrus, Joseph learned that the scrolls didn't survive. He also learned that the thousands of inscriptions on Egypt's temples, tombs, and obelisks emphasized triumphs, not defeats. No one can identify from Egyptian records the pharaohs of the oppression and the Exodus. Tradition said Rameses II, who ruled twelve

hundred years earlier, was the oppressor. His son, Merneptah, was the pharaoh of the Exodus. One of his inscriptions on a stele boasts of a campaign in which "Israel is laid waste"—the only reference to Israel in ancient Egyptian literature. (Nat. Geo. Soc., 110).

Since Joseph was a builder, he was fascinated by the immensity of the structures that he encountered. He spent some time studying one of the smallest of these—a mere 330-ton obelisk built of Aswan granite. He learned a bit about the construction of this monolith, which was a mere speck in comparison to the giant pyramids and massive temples. The little that he was able to learn taxed his imagination almost as much as the work had taxed the muscles of the people who had built this sturcture. The soaring, slender mini-pyramid had been quarried by builders with the use of cantaloupe-sized dolorite pounding stones that were used as hand-held pile drivers. When the stone was freed from the quarry, it was tied to a sled and pulled on wooden boardwalks over the tops of log rollers. Fortunately, there was only a short haul over land and then the longer voyage down the Nile. It took two thousand men working in tandem seven hours to move the polished and hieroglyph-engraved stone five hundred yards to the waiting vessel. Then with hoisting pulleys, they somehow managed to right the stone blade without breaking it and without killing too many workers. However, workers were expendable and replaceable, while monuments to the kings and queens were eternal and precious.

Joseph marveled as he baked under the azure sky and was pelted by the blistering, blowing sand. It was in his eyes and teeth, behind his ears, and under his undergarments. Mary was not as enamored by these pagan monuments. She cringed to think that human ants had reared tombs for titans at Egypt's dawn. It was all too brutalizing, belittling, and unsettling for her to accept, given her tender and sensitive disposition. After the first couple of trips, she was content to stay in the village and tend to her baby. Each day Jesus was growing and changing.

While Joseph found the mechanics and engineering of these projects intriguing, he admired even more the people who suffered and finally were called to liberation in the midst of such monumental feats. Among these was Joseph, his patron among the patriarchs, and Moses, the righteous murderer who transformed his life at the Burning Bush. Moses was no stranger to the grandeurs of Pharaoh's court and the burliness of the taskmasters. Once during his exile after killing a slave driver, he received the divine commission to confront the King. An alien foundling in Egypt himself, he had been reared as a prince. With the royal princes, he surely "sang the writings" at school and copied texts on papyrus and fragments of stone. The words for *teaching* and *punishment* were identical, and a teacher grimly remarked that "the ear of the boy is on his back, and he listens when he is beaten." (Nat. Geo. Soc., 112).

The baby boy, Moses, had been hidden in the Nile River, and now Mary and Joseph were hiding their boy from a murderous plot in the land by the same river. They pictured the scenes of Moses and Aaron confronting the Pharaoh and tried to imagine the ten plagues. It was so unbelievable to think that they, too, were in Egypt, that periodically they had to close their eyes and reopen them to be certain this wasn't merely another dream.

For Joseph, it was a surprisingly easy trip and one that surpassed his wildest dreams. His love affair with his special namesake, Joseph, son of Jacob, seemed to be the secret adrenaline that energized every step of the journey. He had never before seen an Egyptian, but now he felt a surprising affinity with this place and its proud people. In Egypt, the two Josephs' paths met.

The trip that was initiated under a threat to Jesus' life became an exciting and treasured experience. It was remembered as a blessing that seemed to fall from the heavens. Mary and Joseph could only wish that Jesus were older, but that was not the case. Fortunately, Jesus never suffered from colic and was a good traveler. Most nights he slept, and so the village mothers who helped with his care never seemed to feel used or upset. Jesus cried when he was teething, but tantrums were unknown.

A new day arrived and, once again, a dream gave it direction. Herod is dead! The threat is no more! It was time to go back home. Herod had been more than a threat; Herod had been a monster as well as a master of political intrigue who led a life of death-dealing. The Jerusalem herald told the story of his life on that day of his death. His report would be remembered:

"Herod is Dead! Long live the King. What a remarkable creature, that last king of the Jews! Herod was not even of Jewish blood, but an Idumaean—an Edomite descendant of Esau. Scarcely a century ago, the Judaeans had converted the Idumaeans to the Jewish faith by conquest. Herod, with cunning and violence, had eliminated rivals for the throne. He had charmed not only Cleopatra, but successive rulers of Rome. Recognized as an ally of the Roman patrons he flattered, he used terror to control his subjects. An able general, shrewd politician, and excellent administrator, he managed to enlarge his realm until it almost matched Solomon's. His hospitality was magnificent, his works lavish. All over Palestine, and even beyond, rose his temples, amphitheaters, and palaces.

"Herod thirsted for power. Having achieved it, he grew increasingly unstable and suspicious. His own household became a nest of intrigue. In a fit of jealousy, he ordered his beautiful wife, Miriamme, executed. Her brother, the high priest, he had drowned. Sinking deeper into madness, he had three of his sons killed, two by strangulation. When Herod learned of a babe born in Bethlehem whom men called 'King of the Jews,' he ordered the death of all the male children two years old or under in Bethlehem and in all that region. Having clung to the throne for more than three decades, Herod himself finally had died of natural causes. Many people now referred to him as Herod the Great. It's true that he had built magnificent buildings: Greek theaters where troupes performed, the amphitheater where chariots raced, and the hippodrome where beasts tore the life from men. Most of this was an outrage to pious Jews, but one cannot forget Herod; his landmarks stand everywhere: the fine gardens and ponds, the Antonia fortress where troops are quartered, and the palace where the procurator stays on visits." (Nat. Geo. Soc., 196).

The herald concluded, "Herod is Dead! Long live the King." As he ended his spiel, one could almost hear

the commoners and his surviving family alike breathe a sigh of relief and whisper "good riddance."

Now it was time to leave Egypt. Mary and Joseph met with another caravan heading north and were fortunate to find an experienced trail master. The money was running out and they were homesick. They watched as the pyramids became anthills and then disappeared from view. Fortunately, it was the mild season, and the terrain sometimes had redeeming qualities of beauty. Once they saw a broad valley where galaxies of flowers bloomed in response to a recent rain. At other times, they felt like the Bedouin wanderers that they encountered on their travels. These people lived in tents made of heavy cloth to keep out the sun, sand, and wind. Joseph had never seen tents so very large and requiring so many poles in the face of the prevailing desert wind.

This was another time when Mary, Joseph, and Jesus appreciated the kindness of people. The unwritten rules of hospitality that had prevailed since the time of Abraham dictated that asylum be given even to a father's slayer among his victim's kin, and that a stranger be treated as a "guest of God" inviolable when he has eaten his host's food. (Nat. Geo. Soc., 111). At times, though, they would camp at a distance from any settlement. They would prepare for that possible isolation by purchasing dried donkey and camel dung in the villages. That way they would be able to build a fire at night when the evening chill enveloped the desert.

Joseph was a man who unhesitatingly forsook stability and security in favor of fidelity. Once again, he was doing a faith walk, this time with a guide. As he walked along with a homecoming spring in his step, he remembered the highlights of Egypt. He reflected on the great monuments that he had seen and experienced during his visit to this seductive land. He had climbed for thirty brutal minutes under a blazing sun, scuffing against massive sandstone blocks. Finally, gulping for air, he grasped his guide's outstretched hand and stepped atop the Great Pyramid of Cheops, 450 feet above the Giza plain. "You see, sir," the guide smiled, "there is no sight to match it in all Egypt." (Nat. Geo. Soc., 145). Joseph had to agree, and it was unforgettable—just one of the memories that would fuel many a small-town conversation and dazzle his children at family gatherings.

'Magnificent', 'immovable', and 'enduring', were just a few of the words that floated through his head to describe his experience. The builders of these monuments would use the word eternal. As he trudged the same open vastness in which Moses had wandered, he was certain that the spiritual achievement of Moses and his ragged band was mightier and longer lasting than any stone monument he had seen. In the crucible of Sinai, the faith of Israel was forged. As they passed Mount Sinai off in the distance, Mary and Joseph recited the Ten Commandments together. Moses had never entered into the Promised Land. When Mary and Joseph reached it, they would kiss the ground. The Hebrew children of old referred to it as "the land of milk and honey." On their return, it seemed to the footsore Mary and Joseph more like a land of rocks and stones. But it was home, and it had the fragrance of home sweet home. It had not taken them forty years as it had

their Hebrew forebears, but some days they thought it took a decade.

Presentation in the Temple

Joseph and Mary felt energized and eager as they approached the last leg of their journey. But they still had one last stop. They had to visit the Jerusalem Temple. Jesus had to be presented in the temple as the first born who was committed to the Lord High God. In ancient times, families were said to have given their firstborn son to the Lord, but for untold centuries this practice had been replaced by presenting an offering to God to purchase back the first born. Belatedly, Joseph and his family made their visit to the temple and explained the unusual circumstances that had delayed their offering of gift and child. Usually any trip to Herod's Temple, a wonder of the world, would have been a savored moment in a magnificent setting. However, for this travel-weary family, it was merely a command performance. This religious time had become all but a ritualistic duty that was an intrusion on the trek home to be reunited with family. Mary and Joseph even debated whether they should just skip it altogether since it had been so delayed by the circumstances of their lives.

Joseph the Just knew that he wanted to fulfill every detail of the law. Since Jesus had been the product of such a blessed conception and birth, and had been saved from the clutches of Herod, they decided that every demand of the law ought to be fulfilled in regard to Jesus. So they went to the temple as prescribed, but only to fulfill the law, not to sightsee. "Every first born male shall be designated as holy to the Lord, and they offered a sacrifice according to what is stated in the law of the Lord, a pair of turtle-doves or two young pigeons." (Luke 2:22–24). As they purchased their turtle doves from the seller in the temple court, they caught the glances of the hucksters who noticed that Jesus was older than the average child who was being presented. They rehearsed their story of Jesus' life by telling the unusual situations to the boy who was struggling to catch their birds amidst the flutter of feathers in the large cage. He was somewhat simple-minded and interested only in shouting at the skittish birds and venting his frustrations. Mary's and Joseph's unusual plight was not his concern. As he placed the doves in the smaller wooden box with air holes and handed them over, it was clear that he had heard nothing that they had said. Then he added to the frustration by fretting and recounting as he tried to make correct change. Finally, the sale was completed, and they had their sacrificial offering.

Even before they got to the Presentation Station, two pious elders of the temple intercepted them and asked to see their baby. They were kind and caring with Jesus and made all the sounds and facial contortions appropriate to doting grandparents. Mary had often commented to Joseph that nothing energized old folks like a new baby to fuss over. It was her experience in Bethlehem and Egypt and now she claimed it was a universal reaction. They introduced themselves as Anna and Simeon and welcomed the threesome warmly. Both of them were energetic in their old age. When Anna said that her age was eighty-four, Mary couldn't believe it. Mary was pleased to tell her that she had the same name as her mother.

There was a specialness about this chance meeting since they had been away from family for so long. Mary wasn't even sure if her parents were still alive. Mary complimented Anna on her milky smooth complexion that would be the envy of women half her age. Simeon prayed a prayer of surrender that was not to be forgotten: "Lord, now you let your servant go in peace; your word has been fulfilled; my own eyes have seen the salvation which you have prepared in the sight of every people: a light to reveal you to the nations and the glory of your people Israel." (Luke 2:29–32). This testimony to their son's importance was both encouraging and shocking. They wondered whether he had been eavesdropping on Gabriel when he spoke to Mary.

The prophet Anna stood by Simeon's side and praised God in a soft lilting lullaby. Then she intruded on some strangers to show off Jesus like a proud grandmother. When she returned, Simeon spoke this prophecy: "This child is destined for the falling and the rising of many in Israel and to be a sign that will be opposed so that the inner thoughts of many will be revealed—and a sword will pierce your own soul too." (Luke 2:34 -35). The words sounded obscure and threatening, but in the rush to get home, Mary and Joseph would just have to ponder them in their hearts. Maybe at a later date they would understand them.

As they departed from the temple Joseph commented, "While I am itching to get home, I am really glad that we went through with that Presentation ceremony. If we had skipped it, we would never have met Anna and Simeon. In fact, I hope that I grow old with just that much dignity and poise and holiness. Those two are very special." Mary nodded her agreement.

Anna and Simeon were flattered by the warm greeting that they had received from this family. Consequently, Anna and Simeon began to make some small talk. Simeon, a slight fellow himself, joked about the tinyness of the toddler, Jesus. In comparison to the strong, tall, rugged physique of Joseph, Jesus looked malnourished. Some said that unless a stranger knew beforehand that Jesus was Joseph's son, no one would have assumed kinship between them. Later, as people had the opportunity to get to know them both, they realized that Jesus was a "chip off the old block." Neither Mary nor Joseph bothered to respond to Simeon's comment. They knew of no adequate response, and besides, they were in a hurry to leave. They rushed to the edge of town and arrived just as a caravan was forming. The guide welcomed them, and Joseph led his donkey into the line of travelers. Finally they were on the last leg of the journey: north to Nazareth.

Joseph and Mary had given consideration to staying in Bethlehem since they had made such good friends there. But that was only a passing thought since Joseph's children were still in Nazareth. Later they began to hear reports about Herod's son, Archelaus, who had inherited the southern portion of his kingdom—the area of Judea. All of the stories characterized him as being as blood thirsty as his father. That threat ended any fleeting notion that may have momentarily distracted them. Nazareth and their family home never looked so good and they couldn't get there fast enough. The drawn out

journey that had begun with an uncertain first step would bring them home at last.

Return from Egypt

Joseph was heading his little brood back to Nazareth, and the three bone-weary travelers were entering the homestretch with eager anticipation. Their adventure had certainly been full of amazing sights and sounds. They had met more than a few new friends and far too many detours. But now they were returning to family, life-long friends, and home. They had traveled more backroads than they had imagined existed, and the empty, unbroken desert stretched in dreary contrast to the life and color of their Egyptian highlights. But still they were happy, even as they fought off exhaustion. Nearly two thousand years later, Chekhov would write, "Any idiot can face a crisis; it's this day-to-day living that wears you out." For Mary and Joseph—small town homebodies—day-to-day life on the road had been a tribute to their tenacity in the face of tribulations. Through it all, they had their health. And one blessed feature about their return home was that they had been gone so long that the local busybodies had lost count of the days between their wedding and the birth of Jesus. Every dark cloud has its silver lining.

Joseph's children welcomed them back with exuberance and open arms. If any member of the family had given one more hug, his arms might have fallen off. The children were now two years older and eager to meet their new toddler brother. They waited in line for a chance to hold him and snuggle him. There were countless stories to tell, and they all had to be told immediately, resulting in rollicking tumult. Jesus surprised everyone by how quickly he learned the names of his brothers and sisters.

There was a mixture of fantastic travel stories and some somber family news to share. Joseph's sister, Sarah, had died while he was gone. She was the children's favorite aunt because she had never married and was so good to them when their mother died. She had lived a full life, dying at the age of forty-one. Joseph wanted to know all the details of her passing and delighted in relating some of his favorite memories. Mary was saddened to hear that Anna and Joachim had died also. They were such good parents. Most tragically, Joseph's youngest daughter, Rachel, had died in a fall while she was playing. She was climbing a precarious rock formation after she had been told not to go near the quarry. That was the heartbreaking news that cast a gray cloud on the family reunion. Finally, Joseph's eldest son, James, had gotten married and he was in the army. That career was a disappointment for Joseph who viewed it as a sell-out to Roman imperialism. Joses and Judas had done what they could to earn money, but had it not been for the support of their extended family, the children would not have fared very well. Now those hardships were history, and everyone was happy with the prospects for a bright future and the hopes of being a united family.

In the excitement of reunion and catching up with the news, Rachel's death was a shock not to be easily digested. Even after she had been dead for some time, Joseph frequently awoke with this wound as fresh as if she had died just yesterday. It was a Jewish custom to

leave small stones at the gravesite to show that a visit had been made. Rachel's burial mound was covered with pebbles and small stones, one upon another, so that a kind of pyramid was forming. He thought of her often and frequently had to choke back tears.

On balance, Joseph was so giddy with his travels and the wonders of the world that he would never stop telling the stories of the Magi, the Nile, the pyramids, and his Egyptian adventure. Even the tiniest details bore repeating, because they were so different from his Jewish experience. One of the amazing things was the abundance of water that people used with the Nile at their doorstep. There was a ready supply of water in comparison to what Joseph had known. Consequently, Egyptians shaved and bathed frequently. He had been shocked by the worldliness of these gentiles. He had been invited to dinner by an Egyptian trader who had taken a liking to him when he had to trade some of the Persian gold from the Magi.

Joseph described the scene in a story he loved to tell: "Their manor house was designed for light and airiness. They sat on chairs and dined at a table rather than reclining on couches. They could take their leisure in an arbor of the garden, listening to a blind harper chant a love song or an old heroic tale. Wearing their finest regalia and with cones of sweet-smelling ointment on their heads, they had a gala dinner party where each guest was assigned a servant. We were spoiled with generous helpings of the finest food and drink," he would boast with a somewhat mischievous smile on his face. "The high point in the entertainment came with the acrobatic dancers—scantily clad girls specializing in the high kick. (Nat. Geo.

Soc., 114–115). I can't readily imagine how I ended up at such a lavish affair, but I think that my host was certain that I had a stash of Persian gold and that through me he would be able to make important new business contacts. Whatever he thought, I never tried to mislead him and be more than I was. Though the dinner was extravagant and the entertainers were a bit scandalous, I just couldn't get up and leave. Sometimes a person has to be open to the culture and customs of others," Joseph claimed with the air of a savvy traveler. Mary rolled her eyes and joked about how tolerant Joseph was of this scandalous situation. This always got a laugh from the listeners.

On the home front, there was still much work to be done. The boys had done what they could, but many people now wanted plows, wheels, and oxen yolks. They had held off getting these made because they wanted Joseph to do their work. His workmanship was masterful.

Joseph was so busy he had to guard against becoming a workaholic. Mary was satisfied to catch her breath finally and begin to make a home for her family. For a woman who was happy to be a homemaker, her life since the angelic encounter had been a dizzying escapade. The daily chores of the fire, cooking, carrying water, and child rearing were very satisfying. If she were able to spruce up the house for a while, that would be just fine with her. When Joseph wasn't busy with his work and the other children, he contented himself to roll on the floor and tickle, wrestle, and cuddle with Jesus. Sometimes they would laugh so loudly and scream so excitedly that Mary would remind them, "You two settle down. The neighbors will think we've

gone crazy." It was a level of comfort and family seldom available in their nomadic existence.

For Joseph, this was a treasured time to get to know this boy of his who was growing up so fast. One of the things Joseph especially valued was teaching Jesus how to fish. Since he had made him a world traveler before he was two, he now just wanted to sit still with him on the shore of a pond or some stream. Jesus loved to be alone with his dad away from the competition of older siblings. In the beginning, Jesus just liked to skip flat stones on the pond. Then Jesus learned to throw a net. Sometimes they even camped on the beach and fished late into the night. And in the quiet time of patient waiting, Jesus observed the glory of creation in the rocks and ripples, the sunshine and shadows. Finally, Jesus caught a fish that was big enough to keep and feed the entire family. WOW! He was crazy with the thrill of pulling in the net and in knowing that he finally had the knack of it. And after what seemed like an hour, Joseph took the struggling beauty from the tangle and the seaweed as Jesus held the net tight. It was a day of excitement for Jesus. It was a proud day as Joseph taught Jesus his favorite fisherman's prayer:

> "God, grant that I may live to fish until my
> dying day—
> and when it comes to my last cast
> I then most humbly pray—when in the Lord's safe
> landing net
> and I'm peacefully asleep—that in His mercy I'll
> be judged
> big enough to keep."

Joseph prayed it, and Jesus repeated it until he knew it by heart. Then before dinner, they both prayed it for Mary to hear. It was a fish story that they would always cherish, no matter how much it was embellished.

Another activity that Joseph loved was to play a little game with Jesus. He called it, "How much does your daddy love you?" Joseph was always careful to use the most familiar word for *daddy*, "*abba*," so that he could highlight the intimacy of the conversation. He would ask this question of Jesus and then hold his hands six inches apart in front of his chest. Then a few seconds later he would stretch his hands as wide as they could possibly reach. Then he would repeat the question again: "How much does your daddy love you?" When Jesus would point to his muscular outstretched arms and smile, Joseph would say, "Now you show me. How much does your daddy love you?" Then Jesus would stretch his short arms and tiny hands to their greatest extension. When he felt his shoulders pulling at the socket, he felt like he was giving the best sign of all. When Joseph saw this, he would smile proudly. Joseph always wanted Jesus to be certain of his father's love. He wanted him to have no doubts and make no mistakes about it. Very early in life it was clear to Jesus that love had something to do with outstretched arms. The ritual always ended with arms entangled in a warm embrace.

Jesus was eight years old now, and Joseph enjoyed bantering with him. Sometimes they enjoyed chatting with the older residents or having joke contests. One time Joseph said, "Jesus, I don't suppose you know who the straightest man in the Bible is?" Jesus replied, "No, who

is he?" Joseph said, "My old friend, Joseph, because Pharaoh made a ruler out of him." And they both laughed.

Joseph had also made up a story about a man who fell into a well. His name was Kadiddlehopperhausenpheffermachadinahaubernauski. By the time that the word of his tragedy was passed along to the neighbors who might rescue him, he had died. The moral of the story is always to give your child a simple name. Jesus couldn't even imagine how his dad could remember such an absurd name as Kadiddlehopperhausenpheffermachadinahaubernauski. He spent the whole next day trying to memorize it so he could say the tongue twister and pass the story along to his companions. He thought it sounded too funny for words. Finally, Joseph told a story about the return of the delinquent son who returned to his waiting vegetarian family. His dad threw a party for him and killed the fatted cucumber. That was too much! Maybe it was just plain corny, but at breakfast they always joked about the fatted cucumber.

One very memorable day was much less delightful. Joseph was attempting to rebuild the business with his most demanding customers. He had prepared a proposal for a specialty plow and wheels for a wealthy neighbor near the edge of town. Since he was busy, he asked Jesus to take it to the farm house and give it to the family. In fact, it was a nice day for a walk, and so Jesus was looking forward to this grown-up responsibility. He was to deliver some important business documents. It was a parchment with a plow drawing and a price quote. Joseph rehearsed with Jesus. "Knock at the door and say, 'Good afternoon. My name is Jesus, son of Joseph. My dad asked me to come and deliver this job proposal to Isaac, son of Simon. Is he available?'" Joseph explained that if he was not available, Jesus was to give it to the person at the door and ask them to give it to Isaac. "And don't forget to say thank you to the person who takes the package."

Jesus was eager for this task and was proud to be entrusted with this important errand. It seemed easy enough. Jesus arrived at the edge of town and saw Isaac's big house perched on the top of a hill. As he approached, a yellow, mixed-breed hound came charging down the hill at him. He was growling and howling and keeping Jesus at bay. At first Jesus tried to ignore him and kept focused on the task. He held the package over his head to keep the leaping dog from shredding it. But when the dog bared his fangs and jumped at Jesus' face, he turned and ran. The fear factor made Jesus' adrenaline surge, and he barely outraced the canine marauder. When he felt the dog nipping at his heels, he added stretch to his stride. Many people who noticed Jesus' slight stature failed to note his speed and quickness. Once the dog's teeth caught his tunic, but Jesus pulled away. When Jesus was out of the dog's territory, the dog halted and turned to lie under his porch and pant as the slobber ran from between his incisors.

Jesus was happy with his speed and thrilled, content to be alive and unscarred. But he was embarrassed over the failure to complete the task at hand and the fang hole in his tunic. He was still somewhat shaken when he showed the tunic to Joseph. Joseph listened to the tale and was relieved by his escape. "The main thing is that you're not hurt. Your mother can darn the tunic," Joseph said confidently. He said that he had

heard others complain about that dog, and it was suggested that the village require pet owners to keep their animals tied up. "But that probably won't happen until that dog actually does bite some child," Joseph surmised. "When that happens, it will be too late, but then they will do something about that mutt. I'm happy you're all right and that you left when you did. That task wasn't worth your losing an ear or eye to that mad dog. Always remember that people and their welfare are more important than projects."

He told Jesus, "You stay here now, and I'll take the parchment over and talk to those folks about restraining their dog. If you want to make something while I'm gone, use the scrap lumber on the pile in the yard." And as an afterthought he added, "Be careful. And if you use a tool, please put it back where you found it. That way I'll know where to find it when I need it tomorrow." Joseph started down the road and then came back a moment later. "Oh, I'm really sorry that you were so frightened and I'm happy that you weren't hurt. I should have never sent you alone, but I'd forgotten what people said about that mongrel. Be good now, and tell your mother that I'll be back as soon as possible."

Night prayers that evening were longer than usual. Normally the family told a Bible story. Jesus' favorite was the story of David and the giant. Jesus had a hard time at first remembering the giant's name, but he had heard and repeated the story so often that it was locked in his memory. He liked the story because David was the underdog who was tiny by comparison to Goliath. And of course, he came out on top. Jesus got tired of hearing the other kids tease him and call him "Pee

Wee" or "Little Man," so knowing the great story of David was consoling to him. He especially liked the part when the giant's head got bashed in. That was the competitor in him. After the story, Mary or Joseph would lead a litany of prayers, thanking God for the day, for health, for family. They would also pray for certain family members like Elizabeth, Zechariah, and John. Jesus would repeat those prayers after them. Then they would each tell of a situation where God had touched their lives that day. Sometimes a person was touched by the smile of a stranger or the unexpected kindness of a neighbor or the song of a bird. This day Jesus had to recount his whole story of the narrow escape. He was especially grateful that God had given him such strong legs and speed. He knew that he could be the best runner that Nazareth ever had in the popular game called Base. The prayers went on long that night, and so they skipped the song that they usually sang. But they never skipped the goodnight kisses and hugs. They were tighter that night because it had been such a dangerous day. After the family members looked into one another's eyes and said their nightly, "I love you," Mary and Joseph left the candle burning until Jesus' deep breathing signaled that he was asleep.

Joseph and Mary discussed the fact that Jesus was kind of lonely and out of touch with the other children after their travels. There were not many children his age in their village, and since he was so much younger than Joseph's children, he might as well have been an only child. Joseph and Mary invited some of their friends from the pre-Egypt days for supper. They had children whom Jesus was eager to meet. They invited

them to catch up on family stories in exchange for their travelogues. It was an excuse to give Jesus some companionship and a bit of social life.

They were worried that Jesus could grow up a self-centered only child. He might be selfish and not experience much sharing. They knew that one of the ways a child benefits from having siblings is that he or she is forced to share space, clothes, toys, and food. "That is what family is all about," Joseph would proclaim boldly. "If God tells us that we ought to welcome aliens, because we too were once aliens, then children have to start by being welcoming to their own brothers and sisters. And if a child is alone, then we have to develop an extended family. It's as simple as that. Otherwise, Jesus is liable to think that he is somebody and get a big head."

Since the family had been away so long and had traveled so extensively, Jesus was treated with a certain coolness by many of the neighborhood children. The few children who were there had been on their lane for years. They didn't really seem to need "the new kid" and seldom invited Jesus to play with them. In fact, when they were not ignoring him, they seemed to delight in teasing him because he was so small. He seldom was chosen for a team in games. If he was picked at all, he was picked last. The captain who was choosing might say, "I'll take so and so and you can have Pee Wee" as he would point to Jesus. It was the kind of snub that hurt Jesus' feelings.

His dad told him to try to laugh it off and make a joke about it. "Any boy who laughs at you about your size is such a small and weak character that he would find something else to dislike even if you were as big and strong as Samson. He would make fun of your ears or nose or the way you walk and run. Just ignore guys like that and laugh it off. Make yourself lovable. If it gets too hard, remember to say a little prayer now and then for those who belittle you. You might try whispering under your breath, 'Holy One, please forgive them, for they don't know what they are doing.'"

"I guess you're right," Jesus would admit. "But it's not fair, it's just not fair. Why do all the other kids pick on me? I didn't ask to be this small."

"Life is never fair," Joseph tried to explain calmly. "If I had my way, it would be fair to say that I should be the king instead of a craftsman. After all, I'm a descendent of the royal line of David. All of those rotten Roman centurions and governors could just go back home and make room for the real rulers of this land, people like me. Ah, the great monarchy would be restored, and you might be a prince." Joseph spoke those lines with the triumph of an actor on the Greek stage in Caesarea punching his fist into the air to emphasize this royalty. "But," he continued in a small, soft voice, "that probably won't happen, and so we all have to learn to live with undeserved suffering. Everybody experiences some of that. I know that's hard to understand now, but when you get older . . ." Joseph's sentence just drifted off into silence.

Joseph cleared his throat and moved the conversation along. "Jesus, you do have to realize one thing: You are like Mary. You are a very sensitive person who is very easily hurt. You have thin skin like an onion. That means that people hurt you deeply with the

slightest snub or comment. The upside is that you are very sensitive to the feelings of others and in touch with their pain. You can wish that it were different, but that is clearly a trait that you inherited from your mother. You also inherited your size from your mother. So just know that you will have to live with that, and sometimes you will be deeply hurt. All people have a greater or lesser tolerance for pain, either physical or spiritual. Some people get a scratch or pin prick and it's a major thing. They see blood and they faint. Others in a similar situation have a high pain tolerance and so they laugh. That's just the way you are, so make the most of it," Joseph repeated.

Jesus nodded and said, "I think I understand what you're saying, but sometimes I don't like it."

Jesus' sensitivity would come to the fore each time some tramp or beggar would come to Joseph's house for a handout or a meal, or when a neighbor needed some work done on credit. Sometimes he was intrigued by listening to the stories of the travellers who had been to strange and distant places. Sometimes Joseph would play a little game of "can you top this" with his own travelogue, which usually surpassed the visitor. If that happened, it was always done in a cheerful and friendly fashion. Joseph's modest manner won the hearts of every one who came near him. Jesus was saddened to see their tattered clothing and smell the stench of their unwashed bodies, rotting teeth, and reeking breath. Whatever food was available was shared, and if the person needed to stay for a few nights, he was always welcome. These surprise visitors were always welcomed with a smile. Joseph would say, "Even if we have only a morsel to share, we always have a smile to go with it." Smiles are free, and there is no more certain way to assure strangers of our openness and hospitality. Mary and Joseph knew what it was like to be away from home and totally dependent on the generosity of others. In their travels they had known the longing for a piece of bread and a drink of uncontaminated water. Among the regulars who came to Joseph for help, one had a particularly kind title for Joseph. He always called him "an angel in street clothes." Little did he know that Joseph had a better knowledge of angelic wardrobes than most folks.

Sometimes Jesus asked the perennial question: "Why is there so much suffering and injustice in the world?" Joseph's answer was always like this: "God made a world with pain so that we would need each other to get by." One of the things that angered Jesus was when the family made great sacrifices, and the person left without even saying thank you. Once he shared his angry bewilderment with Joseph and Mary. Joseph responded, "Jesus, the truth is that we reach out to help others as a statement of our own need for help. We are all beggars and sinners. We are all in more jeopardy than we dare acknowledge. When I offer bread to the hungry, I am feeding my soul's hunger. When I offer clothes to those who lack them, I am making myself feel more protected from the nakedness of so many moments when I feel that nothing is between me and the devil! When I offer someone a place to stay, I am reminding myself how homeless we all are, unsure on many mornings or evenings of where we belong in God's eyes.

"Jesus," he continued, "it is really we who are the hungry, who are the ones in great need. It is a favor that these people are doing us by coming here and taking from us what we have to offer. I honestly think that it is more blessed to give than to receive." (Coles 190–191). Even as Joseph gave of his possessions, he had to give some serious thought to his occupation. Late at night he would speak to Mary about their situation. Work was slow because timber was so scarce in Galilee, which meant anything made of wood was very expensive. Money was getting tight as the demand for his work declined and their income eroded. The poor lived in adobe houses, and the rich built with stone. Now a new situation presented itself that caused the price of wood to skyrocket. Antipas, Herod's son and heir, was building a new royal capital called Sepphoris—a five-hundred-acre city that would include public buildings, theaters, baths, a sports stadium, and lavish palaces that were the heart of a royal capital. (Varnum). Like all government projects, this was quite extravagant and was driving up the costs of all building materials.

At the same time, the construction of Sepphoris was providing lots of jobs at a decent wage. The new city was being constructed just three miles from Nazareth—a mere hamlet of barely three hundred people that could not offer much work. So even as Joseph's business languished, the job market was expanding.

The building of a royal capital at Sepphoris had a brutal impact on the economy of small-town Nazareth. The construction jobs in the area offered more security than the hardscrabble farming that most people did.

Thus, there were fewer requests for plows, wheels, and yokes. The scarcity of lumber became even more acute, because the demands of Herod Antipas were going to be filled no matter what the price. The law of supply and demand drove up the price of lumber for the ordinary few who tried to stay on the farm. Those people used their equipment longer and did patch jobs to repair their implements and delay the purchase of new equipment. All of these factors caused dramatic changes in the life of Joseph, the village craftsman.

At the end of the day, Joseph would come in frustrated and tired. His weariness was more from make-work projects he did to keep busy than the demands of a backlog of orders. Mary could see the strain on his face and inquired about it. "Oh, it was just a bad day with not much going on," he would dismiss her question with a shrug.

Mary saw that it was more than that. "You know what I think?" she would inquire, then go on to answer her own question. "I think that your bad day is now a bad week and a bad month. I also think that I have to enlarge the garden, because we can't afford to buy enough food."

"Well, what am I supposed to do?" Joseph responded defensively. "Is it my fault that Herod gets all the wood and the local farmers move away? Do you suppose I like sitting around without work or taking Jesus fishing when I should be working? Do you think it's my fault that I lost my knack during the time I was away in Egypt?" Joseph's face reddened and his pitch heightened with rage.

"No," Mary replied in a tender, soothing soft voice. "No, I don't think any of those things. I don't think it's your fault, and I am certain you have not lost your skills. You are an artist at the work bench, but there is hardly any work to do. The construction at Sepphoris has changed everything. I hate to say this because I know how you love your work, but maybe it's time to get a job at Sepphoris yourself."

That suggestion was a hard truth that Joseph had pondered but could never admit. He loved Nazareth and his work-at-home life, but it no longer satisfied. It was becoming clearer. Joseph said, "Mary I think you're right. I've been weighing failure at a job I love or success at Sepphoris. The whole thing has pulled me back and forth like a rubber band, but now I think you've helped me see the light. I was just afraid that you might think I'm a failure."

Mary reached his hand and pulled it around her waist in a warm embrace. She smiled up into his quivering cheeks and said, "Joseph, you will always be my hero and my success story, no matter where you work." And tears gathered in his eyes and trickled down his cheeks and his broad shoulders quivered.

Mary and Joseph prayed about it and decided that Joseph would go off to work in Sepphoris, making the three-mile walk every morning and evening. It was a big change in Joseph's life—one that he didn't really like, but he could still do some small jobs late at night by lamplight. At least there was a way to earn a decent living. Many of the Nazarenes walked together, so there was daily companionship and security. They appreciated the availability of good government jobs.

Mostly Joseph now acted as a mere laborer, but slowly he did learn some of the rudimentary aspects of stone masonry. As a craftsman in Nazareth, he had always had to be versatile, as were many of the artisans of his time. So stone work was not a totally new experience for him. (Nat. Geo. Soc., 330).

After a few weeks on the job, the boss asked him how he liked it. Joseph said it was a good job, and the boss looked on skeptically. He said, "Most new guys say that the first day is the worst and every day after that is the same." Joseph never thought that, because as he toiled he would remember Egypt and tell his coworkers stories about the massive public work projects that had resulted in pyramids, obelisks, sphinxes, and temples that dwarfed the buildings that were planned for Sepphoris. His stories were not offered as bragging, but as a reminder to count their blessings. Their ancestors had built bigger structures as slaves. Joseph would remind them, "It seems to me that we must always remember how well off we are. It is a blessing for us to have such good jobs close to home. We are being paid for our labors. Our ancestors did the work and had to pay for it with their lives." Joseph always liked to couch his sayings in the phrase, "It seems to me." That way he didn't present himself as an expert and egomaniac. He allowed others to have an opinion on the subject, which they could feel free to express.

There were certainly many times when the work was close to back-breaking. At those times, it hardly seemed that the pay was adequate. The grunt work involved in shaping and moving the boulders used on the project enhanced Joseph's statuesque physique

with well-defined muscles. He developed in ways that made him as physically hard as the stone that he shaped. Since he was in peak condition, Joseph discovered that the three or four miles was only a walk. However, all of the workers agreed that it was easier in the morning than in the evening after a long day of work.

Happily, Joseph never got totally removed from the work in Nazareth. Sometimes his job at Sepphoris would call for some specialty items. Joseph got these jobs automatically because his reputation preceded him. It was a blessed day when he could stay home and work. That was always a great perk and a pleasant time of family togetherness. It was also a wonderful opportunity to teach Jesus some of the skills that he loved and valued so dearly. He taught Jesus in the very same way that his father had taught him. "With an adz tucked in his belt, he would proudly teach time-honored skills to his son. He would learn to saw and smooth planks of cypress, oak, olive, perhaps precious cedar; to cut mortises with a smack of stone hammer or iron chisel; to drill with an auger, holding the beam with his feet. He would fashion tables and stools as well as yokes and plows." (Nat. Geo. Soc., 330).

While these opportunities were few and far between, they were always exciting and marked by much delight. When Jesus helped, he leaned toward perfectionism and criticized himself for his mistakes. Joseph tried to show him that to err was human. Finally, Jesus learned to throw his mistakes on the scrap pile and forgive himself.

Jesus Is Lost in the Temple

When Jesus was eleven, Joseph began to think about their annual pilgrimage. While he and Mary had ordinarily gone to Jerusalem for the feast of the Passover, they had never taken Jesus on another trip. Those refugee days were so lonely and stressful that Joseph cared little about taking Jesus anywhere. Mary had a needlepoint that said, "Be it ever so humble, there's no place like home." Due to the frantic pace of their lives, it was never hung—Joseph never got around to putting a hanger on the wall—but it did capture a prevailing family attitude. Now it was time to take Jesus with them, because he was old enough to understand the symbolism of the sacrifice and the beauty of the temple.

Jesus' twelfth birthday was approaching, and the family was getting excited. They would go to Jerusalem as part of a village pilgrimage and family reunion. The travel caravan would have a prayerful and festive spirit. This was Jesus' first opportunity to travel the seventy-five miles to a big city, and he was brimming with excitement. He would see Herod's Temple, a masterpiece, a wonder of the world. He would return to that place where Anna and Simeon had greeted his parents and had become his adopted grandparents.

The family spoke about how wonderful it would be to see them again if indeed that were possible. Anna would be ninety-four. But since she had apparently found the fountain of youth, they would inquire about her at the temple. There was also another hushed dimension to their excitement. No one knew if they would ever have the opportunity for another family vacation. Joseph was not young anymore. The

stonework and the daily trek to and from Sepphoris had taken its toll on him. Many of Joseph's contemporaries had died, and Joseph knew that he was not getting any younger. One thing seemed certain: this time the trip would be wonderful since the family would be together. Joseph said to Mary, "Since our other trips have been difficult, let's promise to make this pilgrimage fun." He made an added request. "In the spirit of a pilgrimage, I think we should dedicate this trip to our parents, whom Jesus never got a chance to know. We'll recall one incident from their lives each day as we travel along. That will make them seem more present to us." It was such a sweet sentiment that Mary agreed immediately. In fact, she thought it was a brilliant idea.

As the pilgrims walked along, they also sang some of the processional psalms. Jesus especially enjoyed the baritone cantor who could sing the psalm "I was glad" in its entirety from memory.

> I was glad when they said to me,
> "Let us go to the house of the Lord!"
> Our feet are standing within your gates
> O Jerusalem.
> Jerusalem—built as a city
> That is bound firmly together.
> To it the tribes go up,
> The tribes of the Lord,
> As was decreed for Israel
> To give thinks to the name of the Lord.
> For there the thrones for judgment were set up,
> The thrones of the house of David.
> Pray for the peace of Jerusalem:
> May they prosper who love you.
> Peace be within your walls,

And security within your towers.
For the sake of my relative and friends
I will say, "Peace be within you."
For the sake of the house of the Lord our God,
I will seek your good.

With the camaraderie and the stories, it was a wonderful trip. The visit to the temple was breathtaking but all too brief. The celebration of Passover was a profound experience of God's mercy and protection. The only flaw in the pilgrimage came on the return trip. By this time all of the travelers had become extended family, and everyone's children belonged to every one else in the party. So it was that Mary and Joseph had traveled one day's journey back home when they became alarmed. Jesus could not be found anywhere. They checked with his brothers and sisters, his friends, their relatives, and the pilgrimage leader. There was only one thing about which everyone agreed: Jesus' whereabouts was a mystery.

Mary and Joseph tried to remain calm and plot their next move. All of the fellow travelers gathered together for their evening prayer. Afterwards, Joseph addressed them all. "Thank you for your prayers and concern. You all go home. Be safe and careful," he urged them as he choked back his tears. "Mary and I will be okay. It's just so hard to imagine losing Jesus now as a twelve year old when we took care of him as a baby in Egypt. I guess those people are right who say when your children get bigger, you have bigger problems. You'll hear from us just as soon as we get home with Jesus. Nothing is more embarrassing," he repeated nervously, "than to travel all the way to Egypt and back without incident and then to lose my twelve-year-old son when he is with family and friends. Take it from a tired old man, the bigger your children are, the bigger the problems that you have."

Mary and Joseph tossed and turned, prayed, and sobbed the night away. At the first hint of dawn, they took leave of their traveling companions and began to retrace their steps to the ancient walled city. This was not the first time that Jesus had been lost. Every child wanders away, and that's not the end of the world in a tiny village. But a teenager lost in a city is something else entirely. That was the real frustration for Mary and Joseph. Jesus had never done anything like this before. He had always been exceptionally responsible for his age. Somehow this seemed like more than just an accident. Maybe he was left behind and it was merely a mix-up in directions. But somehow this seemed contrived. That was their additional worry. Why would Jesus do this?

The moment they arrived in Jerusalem they went to the authorities for help. They told the officer about the inn where they had stayed. They would try to stay there again if a room was available. At least that might be a place where Jesus would return since he knew the owners and liked their food. Joseph and Mary described Jesus to the guards. Now Joseph was kicking himself for not packing the portrait that they had paid a street artist to paint when the carnival came to Nazareth. They had considered bringing it along to show to the other pilgrims, but after further consideration, they thought that the others might think it ostentatious. Maybe it was a bit extravagant for a poor family, and leaving it home was the right decision at that time. But now they thought it certainly would help to be able to show it as they asked around town.

"Where should we start to look? Did he have any friends in Jerusalem?" Those were the guard's questions. "Should we start at the market place, David's Tower, the Pool of Siloam, the Jaffa Gate, or the temple square?" The search would begin with the presumption that Jesus had gotten enough of temple. He would probably be exploring some part of the city that he had not seen on their whirlwind visit.

All of this was so nerve-racking and shocking. Who would ever have imagined that Jesus would pull such a stunt? Even fewer people would have believed that Mary and Joseph would be so presumptuous and assume that Jesus was in the midst of their relatives and friends in the caravan or among his buddies from the neighborhood. Joseph didn't even want to think about that. And then there was his deep-seated fear about this whole matter. It may already be so far out of hand that Jesus would never be found. He shuddered with the memory of Joseph, his ancestral namesake, being sold into slavery. He kept praying, "O Holy One, let him be safe." And then there were the dangers of a large city where children were never safe. Every society has its sick and criminal element. Children are always the most vulnerable. What might be the fate of a lonely child on the street?

Since the guards didn't have a good picture of Jesus, Mary and Joseph accompanied them to the Pool at Siloam and to the various city gates where people gathered to gossip and share the news. Wherever people gathered, there were street entertainers and vendors.

The day's search was futile, and while the sports stadium might have been alluring, it was locked up and empty. No luck. Their hearts sank. Any feeling person who observed their long, downcast faces would have been filled with compassion and suspected that their little world had been shattered. They cried with the psalmist, "My God, my God, why have you forsaken me?"

After roaming about and searching and asking, night fell with more darkness in their hearts than in the heaven. They returned to their lodging for a sleepless night of prayer and feeling guilty. The psalm, "The Lord is My Shepherd," never vanished from their minds. "Even though I walk through the valley of death, I will fear no evil, for you are at my side." They prayed it and it echoed in their ears. They pondered it. They believed it. "Lord, help my unbelief," they whispered in unison.

Joseph knew the throb of splitting headaches on occasion. The pain he felt now was like driving a nail into his brain. Along with that, his whole being cried. His back was stiff, his shoulders ached, his face burned, and his eyes stung. Add to that the press of questions that spun through Mary's and Joseph's heads. Was there something about the special mission of this twelve year old who would save the world? What was his task exactly? Would the God whose Spirit breathed him into life in Mary's womb remove him from the scene without notice? This mystery caused them great anguish. Jesus wasn't born in the flash of a fireworks spectacular, and he didn't glow in the dark. Was the teenage chapter of his life supposed to be more of a spectacle? Would Jesus be mysteriously transported to the Holy of Holies and venerated like the Ark of the Covenant? Were they supposed to be looking for this special child at all? If he is so special, why does he seem so ordinary? Was a search like this only for faithless parents of an ordinary child? This special child was in God's hands anyhow. Should they even trouble themselves? Maybe they should just trust in God and go home quietly. After all, God is his Father; God will provide. These thoughts flooded their minds, and some of them were too troublesome to share. Were any of them true?

In the next minute, the mental debate took a definite turn. Joseph said, "He is our boy, and we have to be responsible. I don't know what dreams and visions of angels mean, but I do know that twelve-year-old boys are supposed to be with their parents and not wandering around Jerusalem. I do know that he is bright and personable, but he still has a lot to learn before he is able to be out on his own." Joseph's comments and thoughts prevailed. Tomorrow they would be out at dawn searching once more. Now they needed to try and get some sleep. Mary and Joseph hugged and kissed. The day had left them exhausted and the darkness left them terrified.

Mary tossed and turned and could only think the worst as she listened to eerie street sounds. Nothing less could even explain how a good boy like Jesus could disappear. In the silent darkness she thought the unthinkable. "To look Death in the face, and not be afraid. That is—Death for myself, but not for Jesus, God, not yet. He's too young to miss all the other parts of Life, all the other lovely living parts of Life. All the wonderful, miraculous things to do, to feel, to see, to hear, to touch, to smell, to taste, to experience, to enjoy. What a

joy Life is." (Gunther 224 -225). Exhausted, her body finally surrendered to a fitful slumber. All Mary wanted was to throw herself down flat, stretch out, and sleep. Tomorrow would come too soon.

The second day was spent searching in the marketplace. For a boy, the Jerusalem Market Square was one-stop shopping under an enormous tent. Should they search by the produce or the candy, the flowers or the food, the clothing or the tools? It was a toss-up. All Joseph could remember was his mother saying, "Whenever something's lost, it could be anywhere." That statement had a more casual sound when the word was some *thing* rather than some *one*. And then if that someone is a child entrusted to your care through an angelic messenger, the stakes are too high to even consider and the sadness is too deep to suppress. It becomes a black hole in the spirit.

Mary tried to share the burden. "Joseph, don't be so hard on yourself," she would say. "After all, I'm Jesus' mother, and I should have been more careful." The words had little effect and fell on totally deaf ears. Joseph could not imagine surviving the treacherous trips to Bethlehem for Jesus' birth and to Egypt with a newborn, and then bungling a pilgrimage with friends. A planned pilgrimage to Jerusalem with a twelve year old should have been an answer to a dream. These self-accusations whirled through his mind and left him so dizzy he had to sit down. The temptation was to quit and go home childless.

The bumping, shoving, and in-your-face hucksters of the marketplace made Mary and Joseph feel like broken field runners on their second day of searching.

They spun, probed, glanced, stretched, and listened for the sound of a familiar voice over the din, but to no avail. It was a place that was so noisy that neither Mary nor Joseph could distinguish a voice. In the midst of the hunt, some of the shopkeepers tried to distract them with the offer of bargains, sales, and specials. They didn't understand that this couple was searching for their child and would have considered the offer of a diamond for a drachma a mere distraction. Sometimes they were tempted to split up and cover different areas in the hope of being more successful, but that proved impossible. Life without Jesus was already too lonely and empty. If something should happen to either one of them, how could the other go on at all? The second day of searching ended in total exhaustion, frustration, and near despair. What if someone had kidnapped their boy? After all, he was a guileless country kid who was totally naive about the intrigues of the city. Joseph and Mary both told each other, "We have to keep our hopes up. We mustn't even think like that."

The next morning, the search concentrated on the temple area. It was only on their earlier arrival with their neighbors that they remembered all the buyers and sellers there. When they began the pilgrimage, they were all hoping to find the temple area more quiet, tidy, and reverent. But soon their hopes gave way to reality. The greed of the money changers sitting at their little tables with scales and the sellers of oxen and sheep, kids and doves, and the stench of the blood of sacrifice were not one bit different from what they had remembered. With the overpowering animal aroma, the odor of incense was barely noticeable. But despite all those nuisance aspects and distractions, there was the awe and wonder of this temple that Herod had built.

Mary and Joseph didn't know where to start. This time they were without a guide and they were hoping to explore every nook and cranny if necessary. After all, their son was lost in this cavernous place. Where should they begin this task?

The temple was located on the eastern ridge between the Kidron and Tyropoeon Valleys, set precisely on the foundations of Solomon's Temple. Here, ten thousand men labored for years raising columned buildings and courts. The temple was girded by an esplanade 550 paces long, four hundred wide, and rimmed by a massive portico. Beyond the esplanade was a railing. Slabs of stone on it proclaim in Greek and Latin that foreigners may go no farther under penalty of death. Through a bronze gate gleaming with gold panels and so large that it takes twenty men to open lies the women's court, which all Israelites may use. Then comes the court of Israel, reserved for men, and finally the priest's court, with its great sacrificial altar. This stands before the temple itself, which rises 150 feet, topped by golden spikes to prevent birds from resting on the roof and fouling it. Over the entrance, facing east, hangs a richly decorated curtain of Babylonian fabric. (Nat. Geo. Soc., 297–298). The size and beauty of the temple was so impressive as to momentarily distract Joseph from the search for Jesus. "Awesome" was the only adequate description.

While the merchants were always busy with their wheeling and dealing, some pilgrims were open to the pleading questions of this downcast couple. Some parents coming to present their first child were attentive listeners. Their own bundles of joy in their arms helped them to be compassionate listeners. "Have you seen a twelve-year-old boy wandering around by himself," they would tearfully inquire. It became harder to ask every time they had to pose the question. The strain of the last two days had made Mary a nervous wreck. It was impossible for this sorrowful mother to appear composed. She felt that sword pierce her heart at the very spot where Simeon had made the prophecy.

Fortunately, they only had to ask the question a few times. One father responded that he had seen a young man among the rabbis and scribes. The boy had appeared to be extremely mature, considering his youthfulness. Mary and Joseph had to shout their thank you over their shoulders as they turned to sprint off in the direction that he had pointed, across the temple portico in the direction of the Holy of Holies. Here, Joseph had to leave Mary behind, because women were not allowed to enter the sacred area.

Joseph entered the sanctuary amidst the dark Corinthian colonnades and porticos. He was perspiring from the run and throbbing with excitement. There in a quiet corner with the sages and respected elders sat their son, Jesus, alive and well! There was a youthful charm about his shiny, smooth complexion in comparison with the bearded, wrinkled faces that dominated the scene. There was a hushed seriousness about the learned discussion that was in progress. Joseph, the craftsman, was hesitant to break into a dialogue that was so eminently profound. He was astonished at the level of questioning and discussion that their young

son found comfortable. It was one of those times when he knew that there was an unexplained wisdom in their child. No small-town rabbi or family discussion had prepared him for this level of dialogue. None of the matters addressed by these teachers had ever come to light in the synagogue in Nazareth. Joseph was mesmerized by Jesus' serenity in the face of all this.

Joseph was delirious. Shivers went up and down his spine as tears of joy welled up in his eyes. He was also anxious to get his hands on Jesus and his arms around his live body. He circled the perimeter of the gathering in a nervous way. Joseph tried to be unobtrusive, but he was calm only on the outside. His insides were relieved, grateful, and seething with anger. How could Jesus be so carefree and aloof while his parents were frantic? Joseph was utterly baffled. Jesus seemed entranced in a totally different space and time zone. He almost seemed separated from earthly life. Somehow, all of Joseph and Mary's frustration and frenzy seemed at odds with the placid demeanor of Jesus. Mary waited outside praying and pacing anxiously.

Finally, Jesus looked up and spotted Joseph peering through the crowd. The laser-like intensity of Joseph's angry stare seemed to jolt Jesus into a present awareness. He waited until an appropriate pause in the discussion and then calmly excused himself from the gathering. Joseph barely restrained himself from darting through the crowd to grab him. When he exited beyond the circle of teachers, Joseph enveloped him with a mighty bear hug. He kissed him and embraced him and squeezed his arms and shoulders. He was real, he was warm, he was alive, and he was going home. Praise the Lord!

Jesus, in his turn, had a quizzical and embarrassed look as Joseph paraded him outside to be reunited with his mother. Even as the reunion was being repeated tearfully with Mary, Jesus was wondering. "What could my parents be thinking to make such a scene out of something so simple? What's their problem? How could they not understand my attraction to my Father's house?" He had stayed at the temple where the Ark of the Covenant dwelt!

Mary said to him in astonishment, "Child, why have you treated us like this? Look, your father and I have been searching for you in great anxiety." (Luke 2:48).

Jesus said to them, "Why were you searching for me? Did you not know that I must be in my Father's house?" (Luke 2:49).

Joseph rushed to Mary's rescue when he saw her wide-mouthed disbelief and misty-eyed sadness stemming from that insensitive taunt. "I'm not so sure what your getting at with that comment about 'my Father's house.' But I do know this much," Joseph retorted gruffly, "as long as you are my twelve-year-old boy, you will be in *my house*." Joseph continued, "Now that's the way it is, and that's the way it's going to be for a long time, young man. Now go and thank those teachers for their time, Jesus, and tell them that you're going home with your parents. Then we're on our way to the inn to get our things and go home."

Jesus returned to the rabbinical circle to explain his sudden departure and to thank the assembled scholars for their patience and kindness. As he traipsed

across the courtyard, Joseph gave Mary a hug and smiled and kissed her on the forehead. It was a forbidden public gesture of affection, and he made certain that they were hidden by a stout column. For their part, the teachers watched with admiration as the bright country boy strolled away with his relieved parents. They saw the trio disappear into the crowd and imagined that the unknown boy, Jesus, would disappear into the mist of time. They would always remember his luminous presence.

"These last three days have been an agony. I sincerely hope that you will learn to like our house in Nazareth and stay there for some time," Joseph was heard to mutter with a great deal more warmth than his earlier harangue. "That is where we plan to be until you grow up. Any long-term visiting to your Father's house in the temple will have to be for another time, maybe another decade. I think that you still have some growing up to do. Thank goodness, you're all right," Joseph concluded with a sigh of relief. That night the family prayed a prayer of thanksgiving with such sincerity as to make all of their previous prayers seem irreverent. However, Jesus still seemed distant, like a teen with clipped wings.

After Jesus was asleep, Mary and Joseph spoke about some of those same issues, questions, and concerns that had barraged their minds a few nights earlier. Who was this special boy anyway? What was God's plan for them? How was God using them to work out his saving plan through Jesus? They still didn't know. All they knew now was that Jesus was safe for another day. Tomorrow they would ask him to tell them more about "staying in his Father's house."

When the question was raised during their return trip, Jesus responded, "I know this sounds kind of ignorant, but I really don't know how to answer. I just felt at home in the temple and drawn to those people like steel shavings are drawn to a magnet." That was the only picturesque answer that Jesus could muster. "Once I was accepted by the group of teachers, there was a mutual respect that developed. I was quiet and thoughtful and asked good questions, so they liked me. And they were approachable, even though there was such an age difference. Most of them were not too stuffy or scholarly but taught in parables. If I get to teach some day, I'll try to use parables. They make so much sense, and understanding them is so easy."

It was clear that he had enjoyed the experience even though he actually seemed a bit baffled by his own behavior. The whole harried ordeal had left them exhausted, but at least they could rest because it was finally over. That night Mary was haunted by the prophecy of Simeon: "Your own heart a sword shall pierce." She did have a nagging heartache. The elegant and awesome temple setting had proven sad and traumatic for them. Joseph sighed and whispered to Mary, "Thank goodness we're all safe." Then he grinned coyly and uttered a new version of the well-known opening psalm verse, "I was glad when they said to me let us go home from the house of the Lord." And they laughed and their eyes danced since they liked their version better than the psalmist's.

Jesus, the Teen and Young Adult

Jesus' wings had been clipped, but his spirit was not grounded. Joseph kept him close at home and saw him develop some significant skills. Even with Jesus' help though, life was still a struggle because of the constraints of the economy. With Joseph away at Sepphoris, Jesus learned to do entire jobs with true craftsmanship. He learned the skill of dealing with clients who are always right. Joseph would stress, "They are our bread and butter, so do everything possible to make them happy."

Frequently Jesus got to do projects alone and enjoyed the challenge of the endeavor. When Joseph landed one of those special jobs, Jesus was there at his side from daybreak until dinner. Once they made a dinner table so highly polished that faces reflected in the surface. When they showed it to their neighbors, everyone agreed that it was fit for a king. But other times, Jesus might wander about in the hills. Joseph knew enough to respect his privacy. Anyone who saw Jesus in these idle moments knew that he had the ability to commune and connect with the spirit of the Creator. While Joseph knew that twelve was not the right age to be in the temple full time, he was certain that Jesus' call would not keep him at the workbench forever.

Joseph had a philosophy of parenting learned with the older children. It was "uncontrolling, but not out of control." He didn't try to keep a leash on Jesus, who loved to walk and visit. But he did want to know where he went and with whom he socialized. Once Jesus had been reined in at the temple, he seemed to be more discreet. Above all, he was more open with his parents.

One day when there was no work, Jesus swept the house while Joseph sharpened tools. Then the two sat down to talk. Joseph cleared his throat nervously and proceeded, weighing each word. He knew that he had put off this conversation too long already. He was so concerned about that phrase, "Father's house." Since things had gone smoothly for some time now, he cleared his throat again and began.

"Jesus, I'd like to talk to you a bit about that horrible time you stayed behind in the temple. First I want to tell you that we all are guilty of some pretty stupid behavior when we are growing up. When I was your age, I got mad at my mother and left home with all the clothes that I had. I spent the afternoon talking to fishermen who were cleaning their nets. When it was getting dark and they were pushing their boats into the lake for night fishing, one of them convinced me to go home. I went back like a scared puppy dog with its tail between its legs. My mother was furious at my disappearance though ecstatic at my safe return. My dad was livid that I had put my mother through such torment. But they forgave me and took me back. So, as you can see, I was not a perfect child.

"We haven't talked much about your disappearance, but I sometimes wonder if you ever got the message that we were terrified. The incident practically killed us." Joseph seemed more comfortable and was happy that he had learned to share his feelings better. "That day when we found you, we were in a dilemma. We wanted to hug you with one arm and wring your neck with the other. And still I am disappointed that you never apologized. I don't think you understood

how devastated your mother and I were during that ordeal. I don't ever recall that you said that you were sorry for all that you put your mother through. She really does deserve more than a glib remark about your Father's house. That was never really satisfactory and seemed more than a bit arrogant. To be truthful, everything that you said just added to our frustration. In fact, after that remark about staying at your Father's house, I was really hurt. Isn't my house the best place for a twelve year old? Am I not a good father to you?"

With that, Jesus broke into tears and apologized profusely. "I'm really sorry, Dad. I guess that I was a bit cocky. All I can say is I'm sorry." He chocked on the words. As he dried his cheeks, Joseph hugged him and then sent him inside the house to apologize to his mother. Finally, that horrible incident was put to rest to everyone's satisfaction. After that honest healing session, the family seemed to reach a new plateau of openness. Joseph was content in knowing that it takes a strong man to be compassionate.

One factor in their lives was the new openness on Joseph's part. He decided that it was also the right time to tell Jesus about their engagement, his dream, and Mary's angelic messenger. These were decisive events in his birth and their marriage. Joseph reminded him, "Remember, I was already a widower and I was planning to marry your mother when she had this strange encounter with an angel. He told her of her special place in God's plan. I began to wonder if she would ever really be mine. You see, once you've lost someone, you're afraid to give yourself to someone else who you might also lose. But I decided that she was the only person for me, no matter what the cost."

A new light of joy and transparency danced in Jesus' eyes, and a peaceful glow transformed his demeanor. This forthright sharing gave Jesus a better understanding of his family and himself. He knew that many of his feelings and life directions were unlike those of his friends, but his parents were unique also. This revelation was a monumental experience for the entire family. It seemed to give him permission to live at variance with a society that was so tradition bound. Joseph had picked the right moment to open the incident for examination and airing. The feeling of peace and understanding, even in the midst of the confusion of divine selection, generated a scene of lasting familial closeness. Everyone got their seven hugs that day.

There was something wonderful and special about Jesus' approach to life. There seemed to be no egotism or selfishness in him. Joseph could only observe and sense his clear-eyed focus and exuberance. Flowers and flies, stars and sunsets, water and wilderness, even a single blade of grass mesmerized this adolescent. There was the sensitivity that Jesus displayed toward people. He especially loved picking wild flowers and surprising his mother with a bouquet. He valued all of his playmates and their parents. Of course, the small town of Nazareth hardly knew a stranger since it wasn't on the main road to anywhere. While one could say that everybody knew everybody, Jesus seemed to share an exceptional level of intimacy. He did not display the casual or arrogant attitude that other teens did. He would listen to the mutterings of the town drunk and converse with the backward and shy. He would pick the

clumsy boy for his team in a game and go fishing with the crippled classmate who walked on the sides of his club feet. Jesus had an openness that allowed him to be spontaneous and uninhibited. Because of his ready smile and self-deprecating wit, Jesus now had countless friends. There was an aura of simple goodness about him that attracted others to his company.

Another thing that Mary and Joseph noticed was that he was extraordinarily good at mediating disputes. He was always able to give situations a humorous twist to cut the tension. And as the son of a just man, he was particularly even-handed. Joseph once remarked to Mary, "If he weren't our son, I would always hope that he would be our friend." Mary shared that sentiment and asked Joseph if he had ever told that to Jesus. When he replied in the negative, Mary said, "Some day you should find a way to tell him your proud observation. I think that would be wonderful, and I'm sure he will be touched." She gave Joseph a wink along with her wisdom.

The family visits to the temple had frequently been overly eventful. The Anna and Simeon experience at the presentation was more than a few idle words from senior citizens. It was both a blessing and a promise of future suffering for the family. Jesus' youthful encounter with the temple leaders was also eye-opening. While Mary and Joseph had seen Jesus as an ordinary youth and looked for him in the marketplace and at the city gates, they had underestimated him. His vision was elsewhere, and his call was higher. In all, Jesus appeared to be a very average boy with above-average intelligence, aspirations, and sensitivity. Some even said that he had wisdom well beyond his years and wondered how that craftsman's boy got so bright.

Just when his parents were beginning to think that Jesus was grown up, they saw once more that he was just an ordinary teen. All of his friends were going to the neighboring village to see a travelling group of performers sing, dance, juggle, and act. It was the first such performance in the area for years. Jesus told his friends that he would be going along even before he checked with his parents. When he mentioned the subject to his parents, they both agreed that he could live without this show. Besides, they knew that the performance would be a magnet for thieves, hustlers, and other criminals. Jesus was broken-hearted that he should be so singularly deprived.

"All of the other guys are going," he proclaimed boldly. "And I have enough money and I want to go. I'll be the only one to miss it."

Joseph said, "We told you that you're not going. Just because you have the money doesn't mean that you have to spend it, much less that you have to spend it on yourself. Now just make up your mind that you're not going."

"That's not fair," Jesus rebutted.

"I thought we dealt with that fair and unfair nonsense before," Joseph replied firmly. "You are right, life is not fair, and sometimes your dear Dad isn't either. Now you have two choices: You can tell your friends that you're not going because you have mean parents, or you can tell your friends that you are not going because you decided to save your money for something better. One way, you blame your parents. That's okay, because we're big enough to take it. The other way, you

take responsibility for your own actions and grow up. Either way, the final outcome is the same. You are staying home and not going to see the show. Now decide what you want to do and how you are going to explain the decision to your friends. The final decision has been made. You are staying home. Now it's your choice as to how you will explain it."

In the end, Jesus shouldered the decision and told his buddies that he had decided to save his money for something better. When it was over, Jesus was proud of himself and found that he had a lot of backbone for a little guy. In fact, half of his friends decided to stay home and have an outdoor party at Jesus' house.

That made Mary and Joseph very proud. Jesus' parents were beginning to appreciate that he was more than they had ever expected. Sharing life with the teenage Jesus was giving them an understanding of a profoundly deep person with glimmers of true wisdom. Besides that, he had a goal and direction: "To do the will of the One who sent him." Everything about him was so big that it belied his small-town experience.

Just when it seemed that the rough spots of life had been smoothed out, another teenage problem erupted. After the Torah class, Jesus and some of his buddies were playing with a little cart that Jesus had built from pieces of wood left over from one of Joseph's projects. Instead of using the cart as it was intended, they were riding in it down the hill on the synagogue terrace road. Jesus was somewhat cocky about this nifty little vehicle which he had built and decided to show off a bit. He launched the cart on a make-shift ramp off the top of a two-foot stone retaining wall on the edge of the synagogue grounds.

The endeavor turned out to be a total fiasco with arms, wheels, and wooden cart parts flying in every possible direction. Hearing a commotion, Joseph rushed over to investigate the wreckage just as Jesus was picking himself up and inspecting his scraped knees, elbows, and chin. Joseph arrived on the scene with outrage and wisdom. Other fathers also greeted their sons with equal measures of outrage and compassion. How could they be so reckless on holy ground? Was anyone else hurt?

While Jesus tried to remove the imbedded pebbles from his burning, bleeding scrapes, Joseph chimed in firmly, "Son, I'm really disappointed by your reckless juvenile display. But most of all, I'm sorry to see you hurt yourself. It's dumb to hurt yourself. One of the things that you have to expect in life is that you are going to get hurt. You are going to be hurt by accidents and by situations that are clearly out of your control. But when you hurt yourself, that is just plain stupid. I hope that today is a learning situation for you. Don't hurt yourself, because you won't have anyone to blame for it except yourself. You are the very person that you ought to love the most and care for the best.

"Another thing that I want to mention is that I really don't approve of one of your friends. Josh is a bit on the wild side and has been accused of several acts of vandalism," Joseph continued. "His older brother has been publicly reprimanded and seems to have a negative attitude. I want to warn you about hooligans like him. You know what they say, 'By their fruits you will know them.' They are bad apples, and I don't think that you want to be involved with them."

Jesus walked away to clean his wounds, clear up the debris of the cart he had demolished, and salve his hurt pride. It was another significant point of transformation in Jesus' life. The incident proved to be his farewell to adolescence. He was about to move into the full responsibilities of his family who had raised him so well. His father was not young anymore and didn't need to face any further complications in life on account of Jesus. He remembered his parents mentioning the Simeon prophecy, and he didn't want to see it fulfilled. If he could help it, Jesus would thrust no more swords in his parents' direction.

One day when Jesus returned to the house after a visit to his favorite cave, he commented about how he enjoyed the sounds and the beauty of nature. Joseph told him something that he had been pondering for a long time. "Remember that Wednesday when your mother and I found you in the Jerusalem temple? There still is one other thing that I want to tell you that was unforgettable. I probably should not have waited this long, but here is a compliment at last."

He continued: "I've heard you talk about how much you enjoy listening to nature. Back on that lucky day when I retrieved you from the crowd of teachers, I noticed how good you were at listening to them and how well you phrased your questions. You had a gentle way of drawing more and better responses out of those men without acting smart. That is really a wonderful gift that you have. I often wanted to tell you how proud you made me feel in observing you. For so long, I was so very upset about that day that I couldn't say anything good. But, finally, here it is; better late than never. You have a way of listening and asking questions that makes people feel very important."

Jesus smiled and replied, "Thank you."

"Let me tell you one of the things that I've learned in dealing with people," Joseph continued. "Everyone wants to feel important. In fact, think of it this way: Imagine that everyone has a sign on his forehead that reads, 'Make me feel important today.' One of the best ways that you can do this is to ask that person a question. When you ask, you are saying indirectly, 'you are interesting, and I would really like to know your idea or feeling about this.' You are humbly assuming that the other person is more interesting or better informed than you are. I tell you, Jesus, take it from your old dad. *ASK* stands for 'ask, seek, and knock.' Asking is an important quality to cultivate. The magic thing is what happens in return. The other person figures that you are so brilliant in soliciting his views that he eventually decides to question you in return. Then real dialogue begins. I've gone on long enough, but I just wanted to say that you will go a long way if you can just sit with people, listen to them, and then ask questions." The conversation ended, but not before Joseph gave Jesus a vice grip hand clasp and a pat on the shoulder while saying, "That's my boy! In fact, I want to add this: even if you weren't my son, I'd always hope you'd be my friend."

Another practice that went hand-in-hand with the annual visit to the temple was the Sabbath time at the synagogue. It had a proud feel because the men and boys always went to a separate area together. Jesus

was among the brightest boys in Hebrew School, and he enjoyed going to learn about the Word of God and the ancient practices of his people. Some of the boys were not as drawn to regular worship and study as Jesus was. When his friends chided him about it, he would say, "Once I'm there, it's not half bad. When I get older, if I have children, I'll make them go like I did." Joseph, his father, was the model of consistency. Certainly nothing was more important to him than fidelity to the Sabbath. So while the other boys occasionally took an adolescent sabbatical from religion, Jesus was dependable. The Sabbath observance was an expectation for all who lived under Joseph's roof. No one wanted to disappoint him.

Jesus and Celibacy

One situation of family life was a disappointment for Joseph. It revolved around beginning to plan a wedding for Jesus. All of Joseph's other children were already married, and he was a grandfather six times already. Sadly, he had also witnessed the infant deaths of three of his grandchildren. But the ones who had survived were quite healthy children, and he was very thankful. He knew that it was his great good fortune to see his children's children. Now there was the question of Jesus' future.

Mary and Joseph had spoken between themselves about a likely wife for Jesus. They had not approached the parents of any of the girls that they liked. In fact they sensed an uncertainty that surrounded this issue, just as uncertainty clouded other areas of Jesus' life. Joseph knew that he should speak to Jesus.

One still night, Joseph and Jesus were sitting outside under the stars after Mary had fallen asleep. The stars were bright, and a tiny thumbnail crescent moon peaked over the horizon. Jesus and Joseph now had a confident openness about their relationship. Joseph began bluntly: "Jesus, I would like to talk with you about your future and plans for your wedding. Your mother and I have considered several lovely girls from good families, but we have hesitated to make any overtures to their parents. There is something so private and reflective about you that we sometimes wonder if you are marriage material. But I hesitate to even speak so foolishly. The tradition tells us that young men are to marry, have children, and pass on the faith. But even as I say that, I can't see you married. There is another side of you that is so open and loving that we really can't see you alone for a lifetime either. In short, your future is a big question mark to your parents," Joseph concluded with a warm chuckle. "So what do you think about this situation? In fact, I feel stupid asking you this question, because everyone gets married. The whole meaning of life is to live on in your children and leave the legacy of children so that you will be remembered. Where are you with all this?" Joseph ended his redundancy, and a long silence ensued.

Jesus raised his face from his hands that had supported his chin and spoke reflectively. "I know that at seventeen I'm at the age to be married and start a family. But I just have to tell you this," Jesus paused to weigh his words and take a deep breath. "I really don't think that I'm supposed to be married. I imagine that you think that sounds bizarre and weird, but it's true. I

know that tradition says everyone gets married and has children and obeys God's command in Genesis. 'Increase and multiply and people the earth.' (Gen. 1:28). But I just don't think that's for me. I think that I would find marriage to one woman and a relationship to one family too narrow and confining. I know that I could do it, but I think that I would suffocate rather than thrive.

"Remember that time when I was twelve and stayed behind in the temple? I really loved those days. I loved being with the rabbis talking and getting to know people in the big city. I trusted your decision to bring me back home, but I don't think that I am called to be a small-town craftsman. And don't get me wrong. I have nothing against small towns, and I don't think that I'm too big and important. And I don't think that our work is too menial. I just know that I have places to go and people to meet. A family and a craft will be too stifling and restrictive. That's the long way of saying that I don't want you and mother to plan a marriage for me. Please don't do that because I won't be right for any woman. I'm not all that clear about my future, but I hope that you will just trust that this is the right thing to do, even if it is unorthodox."

"Trusting and doing what is unorthodox has been our whole life with you, Jesus," Joseph replied with raised eyebrows and a warm grin. "Why do you think that I would be surprised now? The only difference is that previously we had to wait for an angel or a dream. Now I'm getting it straight from the donkey's mouth. It's almost like Balaam's ass in the holy book." As Joseph blurted this out, he couldn't keep from laughing at his own teasing comment.

"So then do you think you're prepared to live a life of celibacy?" Joseph challenged. He paused and cleared his throat even before he said the word that had become so important in his life.

Jesus responded, "I know it's unusual and I think that it is demanding, but some of the Essenes, the ones at Qumran, live celibate lives. They testify that they are trying to live a more authentic commitment to the Almighty. The doctrine of voluntary celibacy is hinted at in Isaiah. (Isa. 56:3–5). It has never been very popular, or the human race would have died out. I don't think that it's easy, but then you taught me not to be tricked into thinking that what is worthwhile is ever easy. Loneliness is another issue. I do think that I will be alone a lot, but that doesn't mean that I have to be lonely. When I make journeys into the wilderness to be alone, I'm never lonely. I feel a deep presence of the Lord Most High within me. I would almost dare to say that I feel a oneness with the divine. Besides that, sometimes people who are married wish that they would have some time alone. And then there are other people who are married who are never really united in any significant way. So being alone and being lonely don't necessarily have to go hand-in-hand. And being married and being united don't either."

There was a pregnant pause, and Joseph knew that this level of dialogue invited a fuller, personal disclosure to Jesus. He cleared his throat, leaned forward on his bench, and looked at the silver stars twinkling in a gray sky. The moon had gotten higher and revealed some wispy white clouds that streaked across the horizon like sheer gauze. Then he looked down and gazed totally into Jesus' face made reddish yellow in the fire light.

"Jesus, let me tell you something I have not told anyone, not even Mary. I know about trust, and I've learned about celibacy ever since you came on the scene. When the angel appeared to me in a dream and told me to take Mary into my home, I thought that I was some kind of a fool. My children needed a mother; that was certain. But I didn't need another child, and I certainly didn't need to move Mary into my home when she was already pregnant. I know that the angel told both of us that you were conceived by the Holy Spirit. I wanted to believe that, but try as I might, I didn't know what that meant. Holy Spirit was a totally strange word. And I must say that you are a good son, but we really have had a boatload of headaches ever since the very first day of your conception. The Holy Spirit in our life hasn't made things easy but they have never been dull."

"Well, Dad, why did you marry Mom if you had so many doubts? I don't get it. You could have called things off from the very first." Jesus' inquiry was clearly challenging.

"Yes, I could have. But I really couldn't have, if you understand love at all. You see, Jesus, I really, really loved your mother more than anyone could ever have imagined. I loved her then, and I love her even more now. So I really wasn't all that free to call things off like you suggest. Love has its responsibilities. You know there is that law about stoning a woman who is adulterous. Now I know we weren't actually married, but the law was interpreted to include anyone who was formally engaged and betrothed. (McKenzie, 14). That included us. So in that sense, it covered your mother. Now I know that the law in Deuteronomy is seldom enforced. But listen to this.

"At the time of your mother's pregnancy, there was a very rigid law-and-order rabbi in town. He was the spokesman for an arch-conservative Judaism called Back to Mosaic Morality. Mary was poor and came from an unknown family. These are always the people who suffer the most brutally when religious intolerance prevails. Capital punishment is never meted out impartially. Poor people always bear the brunt of these laws. Rich people are above them. It's never about fairness; it's always about making some poor person an example of a community's high moral standards. Now you know the whole story about our marriage. It was a real cross to bear in the beginning, but it became my greatest joy. In a nutshell, I married your mother because I loved her so much as to protect her from the brunt of a savage law."

Joseph continued: "I remember once when I was very small seeing a woman caught in adultery stoned to death. It was a horrible sight that took my breath away and then caused me nightmares for the longest time. I have flashbacks and can still see it vividly in an instant if I don't consciously block it out. And it still makes me sick. The whole thing was mob madness. And after the first person pitched a pebble, the violence escalated and was vicious and barbaric. Finally, when the girl was bloodied and unconscious, some 'pious' men dropped a boulder on her. That crushed her face and put her out of her misery. From the instant that the havoc broke out, I just wanted to shout: 'Let the person who is without any sin at all cast the first stone.'

Instead I was silent. I don't think that my lowly voice would have made any difference. No one seemed to be rational, much less sympathetic. An angry mob is not a pretty sight. That's why I always told my children if you're tempted to do anything wrong, do it alone. It's much harder to be evil all alone. You won't get into as much trouble without a gang to goad you on."

Joseph paused. "So I knew that I didn't want Mary to face that kind of horror. Whether she was pregnant by the Holy Spirit or not, I knew that I loved her too much to see her exposed to the full force of that brutality. In her case, there would be no scales of justice; just a deck of cards stacked against her. So I took her into my home and said nothing to anyone. I wanted to believe the story about the Holy Spirit even though I didn't understand it. My own dream made the situation more credible. It made my difficult decision more palatable. Of course the longer we were together, the more I realized that my initial love for Mary was really just a fragment of the love that has developed over the years.

"Another thing that was exciting and reassuring was her trip to visit her cousin, Elizabeth. In my imagination, I could envision a thousand reasons why that trip was too dangerous and out of the question for a pregnant teenager alone. I must say that your mother is quite a trouper. When I saw that she really wanted to make that trek, I knew that she believed the story she had heard from the angel. Then, when she returned with stories of the new baby and the healing of Zechariah's tongue-tied condition, it was reassuring for me also. The truth is, I think we both needed the guarantee that John's birth offered."

There was a long, heavy pause, and then Jesus responded with a sigh of relief. "Wow, that was really traumatic. I never knew that story and couldn't have imagined the law of stoning being applied in our family and to my own mother. Dad, you are really quite a man. No wonder people have always called you 'The Just One.'"

"I'm glad that you feel that way about me, Jesus. But I just hope that I measure up to the holiness and strength of your dear mother, Mary. Whatever you might be able to say about me, you can say about her twice over. I have been blessed with a wife who is very faithful to God and who is a dear person. She is a person who hears the word of the Almighty and keeps it. Like that time we found you in the temple, and you said you had to be in your Father's house. We didn't get that, but she just pondered it and prayed about it. One thing is for sure: Being the parent of a teenager certainly promotes praying." Joseph interjected his comment with a chuckle. "Another thing is certain about Mary: Once she faced the threat of stoning, she became a strong advocate for the poor. She is a person who believes that the Creator loves people no matter how lowly they are."

Jesus rose from his crude stone bench, reached out to embrace his dear Dad, and pull him to his feet. It was the role reversal of the forgiving father and the prodigal son. Jesus was no longer the runt, but had filled out and firmed up after an unexpected adolescent growth spurt and his periodic employment at the Sepphoris project. Now he looked like a man accustomed to hard labor. He embraced Joseph in a crushing embrace. It was the mother of all bear hugs. Tears from both their

cheeks mingled and disappeared into Joseph's ample beard. They lingered together until their arms were tired. When they withdrew from each other, they each dried their eyes with the flowing sleeves of their tunics. Once again, Jesus sat down, and Joseph stood as if to make a special point.

"Well, Jesus, it's nice of you to say that I am quite the man, even 'The Just One.' But I don't have anything on your mother. Now there is one strong woman whose middle name should be *Yes*. She was a mere teen when she said 'Yes' to the angel. She knew she might be the subject of town gossip and ridicule. She knew that she might be convicted of a capital crime, but she knew that it was more important to be obedient than to be alive. She chose to conceive and bear you no matter what the cost. And she had the chutzpah to ask the angel how this was to come about since we had never been sexually intimate. Her generous response to the angel took unparalleled courage. She is a spiritual iron woman. I can't begin to tell you how proud I am of Mary. She is some woman, my wife and your mother. She is God's chosen.

"First, she risks death by stoning. Then she risks death on her trip to Elizabeth's house in Ain Karim. Then she risks death on that trip to Bethlehem when she is almost nine months pregnant. She didn't have to go because women don't count. The village midwife told her not to go with me, but since we had been separated almost since the first day of our marriage, she wanted to be with me. Not only is she courageous, she is also holy with a capital H. Pregnancy is demanding enough. All of the children that my first wife had were born at home. We had a community of support. But

Mary handled it. Really, we handled it with lots of prayer. Parenting promotes praying, it teaches praying and, in fact, it almost forces praying. I must say, Jesus, that your entry into this world marks your mother as the ultimate hero. (Cunneen 49–50).

"There's one more thing that I want to tell you about your mother now that we are having this heart-to-heart talk. Your mother is without doubt the most prayerful person in the world. She lives her life paying constant attention to the unexpected inspiration of the subconscious and the angelic. Often times over these years we have been afraid or unprepared to believe in some impossible future presented to us. But Mary was so transparent and so in tune with the Almighty, that she was able to walk in faith trusting in the future. The angel told her on that first visit that all things are possible with God, and she has always believed it. What a woman of prayer she is!"

When he appeared to be finished, Joseph began anew, clearing his throat as if to make the most important point of all. "When Mary came back from Elizabeth's house, we spoke about the fact that she wanted to remain a virgin totally open and available to the Holy Spirit. I, for my part, already had a family, and I wanted to live a celibate marriage out of respect for Mary's special divine calling. I had been thinking about this and praying about it during her visit to Elizabeth. The image that kept coming to my mind was the great story of Moses and the Burning Bush. Moses was attracted by the Burning Bush and went over to investigate the phenomenon. As he approached it, he heard the All Holy One call to him. 'Moses, Moses!' And he said, 'Here I am.' Then he said, 'Come no closer! Remove the sandals from your feet, for the place on which you are standing is holy ground.' And Moses hid his face, for he was afraid to look at the All Powerful One. (Exod. 3:4–6). I have to tell you that I felt like my relationship to Mary was similar to Moses' situation at the Burning Bush. I felt that I was being told to 'come no closer.' A life with Mary, the specially chosen, was too much for me: too blessed, too holy, too unspeakable. In comparison, I was such a nothing. I said those words, celibate marriage, to myself and then to Mary, and we both agreed. I still can't honestly say that I knew what this type of life actually demanded, but then all of life is a mystery, and you never know the future demands. We decided to live our marriage without sexual relations. We knew we would have to approach it humbly and do it one day at a time.

"Sometimes that was exceedingly hard, and at other times—more often than I could have anticipated—it was easy. Love can make the impossible possible, even easy. That's because we loved each other so much. One thing was certain: Celibacy was hardest when we were distant or out of touch. We needed to be bound together by daily prayer and daily caring. We always needed to be warm and intimate with each other, but not sexually united. It took practice, and sometimes we came dangerously close to breaking our commitment. Fidelity was the hardest when we had money problems and I had to work at Sepphoris. But then God sent angels to watch over us and save us from our worst selves. One of the things that you have to know is that there are temptations to lure you no matter what your life commitment is. Single people are tempted to fornication, married people are tempted to adultery, and celibate people are tempted to sexual activity. All of those flaws are equally tragic because they are broken commitments. They are abandoning the excellence of our best selves and our love of the Most High. Thank the Lord, Mary and I were able to keep our commitments because of our balanced lives and supportive friends. We were especially blessed by those in the synagogue who shared their lives with us. They laughed and cried with us and mourned and celebrated with us. And when the stresses and pressures got to be too much, I went fishing." Joseph concluded with a knowing smile and a right thumb up. "Do you remember that Fisherman's Prayer I taught you?" Joseph laughed and almost woke Mary.

After a ponderous silence, Jesus responded. "When you said that you had to be warm and intimate with each other, I knew what you were saying. I always noticed that the two of you were much more complimentary and kind to each other than many of my friends' parents. You always seemed to notice the attractive qualities about the other. You never seemed to take the small things for granted either. So many of my friends are more interested in their possessions and in their achievements. They seem unaware of inner beauty. You and Mom always seemed to be conscious of the spiritual life and the other person. That's really impressive. Some of my friend's parents are married singles. When I am with surfacey people like that, I can feel them suck the life and energy out of me. On the other hand you have depth, you exude life."

"Well, Jesus, I'm happy that you noticed that," said Joseph, "because we decided from the very beginning that those qualities would be the only ones to make our celibate marriage possible."

"That is just what I needed to hear, Dad," Jesus replied with a sigh of relief. "That is the reason why I think that it will be best for me not to marry. I just want to be a bit more of a free spirit—not in a pleasure-seeking way, but in a truth-seeking fashion. I am confident that I will be able to do it. You and Mom have been a great example for me."

The embers in the courtyard fire were barely visible through the fragile white-hot ash. The night was disturbed by the cock crowing off in a distance. Jesus and Joseph's dialogue had drifted off into prolonged silence. Neither was aware of how late it was. Finally, Joseph rose and as he walked toward Jesus, he too stood up. They embraced once again, this time feeling their bodies expand and contract with each breath. The words of that evening were now silent, but they were emblazoned in the minds and hearts of both speakers. The crickets chirped as Joseph and Jesus returned to the house where Mary's heavy breathing and deep sleep gave way to a restless turn and a deep sigh.

Later that week, Joseph seemed to continue in that pensive and spirit-driven direction. Whenever talk strayed from the job at hand, Joseph warned friends and neighbors in passing conversation about the dangers of letting their spiritual lives get flabby. He would say, "It seems to me that the holy word and the practice of listening to the Lord and his teachers must take priority over idle gossip and chatter. There will always be a tension between coziness and character. And wise people will always choose character." He would also remind those who were willing to listen about the prevailing necessity of an attitude of gratitude. "Moses warned us: When you are richly blessed in the land that I will give you, you are just likely to forget the Lord and think that you earned what you have by your own hard work. If you want to know the truth, all of life is a gift. Nobody pulls himself up by his sandal straps. And I'm the most blessed and gifted of all." He would tell himself in a hushed whisper, "When I am in Abraham's bosom, I just want to ask one question: Why did you love me so much?"

Joseph, Hope of the Sick

Merciful Saint Joseph, you are the hope of the sick, for you have at hand the almighty healing power of Jesus. Through your intercession, one may obtain almost any favor compliant with the will of God. Hear with kindness my prayer on behalf of all those who are ill and who are suffering.

I beg of you to request Jesus to alleviate the sorrow and pain of the person I especially recommend to your attention by obtaining the grace of a patient submission to God's will, a prompt recovery from illness, and the favor of leading a life in full harmony with the Gospel teachings and the inspirations of the Holy Spirit.

O Saint Joseph, let not my prayer go unheeded, but through this urgent request help me to intensify my feeling of gratitude to you and to our heavenly Father. Amen.

Saint Joseph's Oratory of Mount Royal
Montreal, Canada

5 The Death of Joseph

Jesus' life was formed in the arena of love, family, prayer, solitude, labor, and community. In short, the family of Mary, Joseph, and Jesus lived life passionately. Other families may well have had more of this world's possessions, but none of them had more of the values that produce happiness. In terms of material things, there was always enough but never an abundance. Joseph would frequently lead the table blessing at dinner thanking the Lord "for making us the richest family in the whole world." There were times as a boy when Jesus believed that they were wealthy. After all, his dad was a craftsman and they always had food on the table. At the same time, it was obvious to all their friends that, despite life's stresses Joseph was a contented man. He would say, "Accumulate friends rather than possessions."

Joseph was one of those fortunate people who retained his youthfulness well beyond his actual years. Then it seemed that a day arrived when Joseph was old. Suddenly, he had wrinkles that chronicled his wisdom as well as his years. He was still strong, but stoop-shouldered, and in failing health. His other children had long since grown up, married, and moved on. As

life-long Nazarenes would have predicted, the strong, angular Jesus, the child of his old age, was now the town craftsman. He was at Mary's side to see to Joseph's comfort and care.

On a particularly dark and still night, Jesus and Mary stood by Joseph's bed. He had been ailing from a cold and then a fever and achiness. One bad day of malaise slipped by—then three days, and soon a whole week of feverish, halting sleepiness. Each day seemed a bit more taxing. His appetite was gone and his strength went with it. However, his mind was good. People who saw him less frequently noted that his complexion was like veal, and liver spots marred his face and hands. Despite this, his face was still serene and peaceful.

During one of his last nights, he had a dream or maybe a nightmare. It was as vivid as any of the many important dreams that had preceded it. In this dream, he saw Jesus as a grown man—beaten, battered, hissed at and booed at, and carrying a cross like a notorious criminal. Crucifixion was the worst form of torture. The Jesus of this dream was severely beaten almost beyond recognition. In fact, Joseph recognized him only by the gait of his walk. The brutality of the scene was heightened by a crown of thorns on the top of his head. He saw him nailed to that crossbeam and then saw it raised and placed in the groove of the upright that was planted firmly on a hill top. Joseph had never seen a crucifixion in his lifetime, but he had heard stories from others who had witnessed this supreme act of Roman barbarism. As ugly as this dream was, there was a facet of it that caused Joseph added consternation and concern. The clearly printed sign nailed to the top of the cross over

Jesus' head read simply, "Jesus of Nazareth, King of the Jews." After that the dream lapsed into blackness and blood-curdling, cacophonous chaos. It was a head-splitting experience far surpassing any he had during the time when Jesus was lost in Jerusalem. He wondered if this was the horrid side effect of a potion a neighbor had prescribed for his relief.

Fortunately, there was a final segment of the dream. In it Joseph saw Jesus alive and walking around with some people who seemed to admire him greatly and rejoice in his new life. While his nail marks were still clearly evident, he appeared surprisingly healthy, strong, and radiant—almost aglow. Joseph didn't know what to make of that startling dream, and the happy ending barely redeemed the terror of it all. He decided that he would never want Jesus to get an inkling of this and that he could never share this dream with anyone but Mary. It would just have to be their secret, and in the sharing of it the burden was lightened. Maybe Mary could help him to understand it even as his days were growing fewer and his mind was fading. Joseph liked to think that there was not anything to it but hallucinations from the wrong drug. He stopped the medications and never had a recurrence of the nightmare.

Mary and Joseph spent hours recalling the dreams, struggles, and satisfactions that had made their life together worth living. They chuckled about the many predicaments they had faced. With the dangers of foreign travel, Joseph knew that it was a blessing to die in his own bed. Joseph and Mary agreed that their vow of celibacy had periodically seemed impossible. But they had been faithful, and they were thrilled with the love that they shared.

If one word could sum up Joseph's life, it was *satisfaction*. He was satisfied with his marriages, with his children, and especially with Jesus, the child of his old age. He was satisfied with his work, with his religious practice, and with his place in God's plan. He still delighted in his travel memories and the diverse friendships these brought him. Most of his contemporaries had never traveled farther than Sepphoris or Jerusalem. He was satisfied that although he and Mary had often been faced with threatening uncertainty, they had always survived. "And," he would say, "when you survive with love, family, and with God, you really do thrive."

Mary and Joseph would punctuate their litany of blessings with a shared smile, clasped hands, and a kiss. Then when Joseph reached a time of extreme tiredness, Mary would massage Joseph's back, shoulders, and feet. There was even satisfaction in knowing that they were wise enough to know when enough is enough. They wanted to pause occasionally in the midst of counting their blessings and say the phrase from the Passover meal, "It would have been enough." Even if they had little and had been denied more, what they had was always enough.

The time for talking and remembering became more labored and was frequently interrupted by sleep and mental lapses. In the waking hours, many half-forgotten family situations came back to mind in vivid detail. Each of the children had his or her favorite story. Sometimes stories were shared in private when each person was able to tell Joseph of her/his gratitude and love.

Jesus' special memory was the time that he caught his first fish. He remembered the prayer that Joseph taught him at the time and had prayed it often. He thought that the excitement of that day made all subsequent fishing trips special memories of his father Joseph. It was a time of bonding that he would cherish forever. He only wished that they had found more time to fish together. He promised Joseph, "When this is all over, I'm going fishing for an entire day. I will spend all of my free time fishing and thinking of you," he said with a teasing grin on his face, but with sad eyes that glistened with unspent tears.

"On a more serious note though," Jesus continued. "There is another thing for which I want to thank you. I want to thank you for being a person of such great integrity in every aspect of your life. I think that the best thing that I can say about you is that your words and your actions were always in accord with your faith in God. I just can't thank you enough for such invaluable openness. I know that you're not perfect, but you and Mom are the most perfect people I have ever known. You were most perfect when you admitted your mistakes." And with that comment he leaned over and kissed Joseph on his forehead.

Jesus and Mary seldom left Joseph alone, so each had some quality private time to thank one another for the blessings they had shared as a family. All of Joseph's children visited, and some of them were reconciled who had been alienated in the past. One of them spent years struggling with the sense of abandonment that he suffered during that long two-year absence in Bethlehem and Egypt. Sometimes they would pray as a family or sing songs. Sometimes they would laugh. Other moments were times of somber waiting and unabashed sorrow.

Sometimes Joseph wanted to just be alone with his own thoughts. Frequently, they were his memories, but even more likely these silent times were times of prayer. Joseph particularly liked the prayer that Simeon had prayed decades before at the presentation. He could never remember it all, but he could never forget the old man's gentleness and serenity as he spoke the opening sentence. Joseph appeared to be much smaller now. With great effort he raised his voice and gestured, pointing up to the sky. "Now, Lord, you can dismiss your servant in peace according to your word." So many of the things that Anna and Simeon had spoken were eerily prophetic at the time. Later they gave greater meaning to life. Joseph was grateful for that. He cherished another prayer, which in the end he spoke in a barely audible tone. "From the unreal, lead me to the real. From darkness, lead me to light. From death, lead me to immortality."

Jesus and Mary held his hands and stroked his brow and moistened his lips as Joseph slipped into sleepy incoherence. As the breathing became more labored and shallow, he exhaled and gave up the spirit. He slept away in peace. In fact, the end was so peaceful that Mary and Jesus had to study Joseph's chest and abdomen for some time to make sure that he had breathed his last. As his skin began to gray and his lips turn blue, they were certain that his giant lively spirit had departed from his energetic body, leaving it a mere shell. Death had come like a candle blown out by the breeze. It was the kind of peaceful death that fulfilled Joseph's deepest wish. His light was extinguished as the sun crept above the horizon and a new day was just beginning. Jesus and Mary fell into each other's arms and sobbed gently at a loss that had pierced their hearts. The entire family came together in a group embrace. What a good husband! What a dear father! Some held each other and sobbed, while others went off to be alone. "The dust returns to the Earth as it was and the spirit returns to God who gave it" (Ecclesiastes 12:7).

The family spent the morning preparing Joseph for burial. There were no undertakers in Nazareth. One thing that everyone understood was that washing and clothing the body was the final and highest act of kindness. It was the final treasured gift of self that could never be repaid. It was total and selfless generosity. Each of Joseph's children took turns sitting silently with Mary and praying, while other children washed the body of Joseph on the bed where he had died. Then they prepared it for burial.

One of Joseph's last requests was to remind the family of the oldest and most valued treasure that they possessed in their humble home. That was the myrrh from the kingly visitors at Jesus' birth. While the gold from the Magi had financed their trip to Egypt and helped them over some rainy-day rough spots, and the frankincense had been presented in Jerusalem to be burned at the temple, the myrrh had been preserved in its original polished wood box. Joseph never forgot the excitement of that surprise visit. Over the years, the family members had frequently teased him about the fact that he probably loved the beautiful box more than the expensive gifts that wooden box contained.

Now was the time to remove that red aromatic gum resin from its treasure chest and make it a liquid by mixing it with olive oil. The pleasant fragrance of the mixture quickly filled the house and mingled with the smell of the lilies growing outside the window. Each of the children took turns with the ritual of anointing the body with the myrrh and oil and giving it a final tender touch as rigor mortis set in. One of the tasks that Jesus treasured was that of bandaging Joseph's hands and feet. (Nat. Geo. Soc., 306). He wanted to be the last person to caress those hands that had worked with his own and taught him his craft. Joseph's aged and wrinkled face, marked both by suffering and smile lines, was then covered with a cloth before the linen shroud was pulled over his entire trim body that still showed the sculpted muscle lines of a vigorous life. Mary observed her children proudly, frequently holding Joseph's hand or stroking his forehead and smoothing his hair. She gave the final nod of approval to their work and wrapped Joseph once more in her loving embrace.

Soon the word of his passing was broadcast via the morning grapevine at the town well. The funeral that afternoon was not lavish. There were no formal ceremonies, just a simple burial in the Nazareth cemetery. The cemetery was actually an abandoned cave on the edge of town. Centuries earlier it had been used as a sheep shelter, but now it was used by almost everyone except the rich. It was a lovely, quiet spot far away from the main road to Capernaum. It was a fittingly simple way to mark the end of a simple life for Joseph the Just.

There was never anything ostentatious about Joseph's life. His funeral was as unobtrusive as the man himself. He was laid on one of the rough-hewn shelves that marked the inside wall of the darkened hollowness fifteen feet back from the entrance. The fit in this bunk-bed-style tomb was tight, and it was difficult to place Joseph straight on the narrow shelf. One of the more impetuous pall bearers lost patience and in frustration retreated into the entrance chamber. Another reminded the others that this burial act must be done properly so that Joseph would be flat on his back to await the resurrection, "whatever that really is," he added in a bit of a questioning mutter.

Another pall bearer was overheard speaking to his own son as the huge round stone disc was rolled down the rutted groove in front of the yawning cave entrance. "Joseph the Just was the richest man in Nazareth," he said convincingly. As his son looked at him questioningly, he was quick to add, "the wealthiest man among us is the one who is the best. Joseph was God's best man!"

Appendix

Sources

The oldest interpretation, which is to be found with the Early Fathers, still lives on in the Oriental Churches, including the Greek Orthodox. According to this tradition, Joseph was a widower when he took Mary to be his wife. His first wife bore him four sons and two daughters. Mary had only one son of her own but raised all of the children and was greatly esteemed by all as their mother. This interpretation goes back to the *Protevangelium of James*, written in the second century. It certainly contains many additions. But its ascription to James, the Lord's brother, allows one to assume that it also contains authentic family records. The tradition that the Brother of the Lord means half-brother may belong to such a category.

The discovery of the Dead Sea Scrolls near Qumran has given new access to and a better understanding of the events that could have led up to the birth of Jesus. According to the oldest sources, the words of Mary to the angel at the Annunciation—"How will this be, since I do not know man?" (Luke 1:34)—are interpreted to mean that Mary felt herself bound by a vow to continence (chastity). Experts on present-day rabbinical Judaism and the pharisaical Judaism of the Second Temple period maintain that such a behavior could not be Jewish. In the Pharisaic view, the very first duty of a person is to marry and to have children to ensure the continuation of a family line.

But today we know that some Jews who were influenced by the Essene school thought differently. In the Temple Scroll, which was found in one of the Qumran caves, opened after the Six-Day War and published by Y. Yadin, the following instructions were found: "If a girl takes such a vow of continence without her father knowing about it, the father then is entitled to nullify it. Otherwise both are bound to keep it. Should a married woman take such a vow without her husband knowing about it, he can declare such a vow void. Should he, however, agree to such a step, both are bound to keep it."

Could not both possibilities apply to Mary? Mary's father then could have entrusted her to a man, who was prepared to acknowledge such a vow. Seeing that the widowed Joseph of the Davidic line already had children, he could have found it easier to agree. The family *haggadah* of the *Protevangelium* sees it essentially like this, even though many details in it may be sheer fantasy.

So the great astonishment of Joseph, who was regarded by his neighborhood as a *tzaddik*, a righteous man, also becomes understandable. In the Jewish community, a *tzaddik* is a faithful observer of the law. Was not his oldest son James the leader (bishop) of the first messianic community of Jews in Jerusalem, who carried the name Tzaddik James the Just? This is surely a title that both could have earned by their conscientious observance of the Torah. (Pixner, 51–52).

Bibliography

Brown, Raymond E. *The Birth of the Messiah*. Image Books. Garden City, 1979.

Carroll, Patrick L. and K.Dyckmen. *Chaos or Creation*. Paulist Press. New York, 1986.

Coles, Robert. *The Moral Life of Children*. Houghton Mifflin Company. Boston, 987.

Cunneen, Sally. *In Search Of Mary, The Woman and The Symbol*. Ballantine Books. New York, 1996.

Gunther, John and Frances. *Death Be Not Proud*. Harper Perennial. New York, 1989.

Levy, Jacob. *Wörterbuch über Talmudim und Midraschim*. Berlin, 1924.

McKenzie, S. J., John L. *Dictionary of the Bible*. The Bruce Publishing Co. Milwaukee, 1965.

McRoberts, Omar. *Soulfires*. Daniel J. Wideman and Rohan B. Preston, editors. Penguin Books. New York, 1996.

National Geographic Society. *Everyday Life in Bible Times*. Melville Bell Grosvenor and Frederick G. Vosburgh, editors. Washington, DC, 1967

Pixner, Bargil. *With Jesus through Galilee According to the Fifth Gospel*. Corazin Publishing Co. Rosh Pina, Israel, 1992.

Varnum, Paul D. *That the World May Know*. Focus on the Family. Colorado Springs, 1996.